DATE DUE
BIG S F 1 0 1
MONTA J 1 1
SEIAD C 3 1
DELPH B 9
00
D0436416

Poppet and I
(*Copyright Tony Travers*)

STARTING FROM SCRATCH

Jeannette Travers

Taplinger Publishing Company
New York

First published in the United States in 1976 by
TAPLINGER PUBLISHING CO., INC.
New York, New York

Printed in Great Britain

Library of Congress Catalog Card Number: 75-37390
ISBN 0-8008-7369-6

To Tony, whose deep concern and compassion
for animals made this book possible.

Acknowledgements

My especial thanks to Tisha Browne for all her valued advice and encouragement, so generously given.

My grateful thanks to Felipe Benavides, Peru's leading conservationist; Dr. Michael R. Brambell, London Zoo; The British Council, Lima, Peru; The British Council, Mexico; Frank and Helena Farrar, Colchester Zoo; W. J. (Bill) Jordan, R.S.P.C.A., for all his valuable help, which is very greatly appreciated; Long Island Ocelot Club, U.S.A.; John Knowles, Marwell Zoological Park; Reg and Pam Matta, Suffolk Wildlife Park; Roger Wheater, Edinburgh Zoo; Neville Whittaker, R.S.P.C.A. London Airport; and to our animals' marvellous and dedicated veterinary surgeon, to whom Tony and I are deeply indebted, especially for his superb treatment and understanding of Poppet Leopard.

Chapter One

"Let's have an ocelot," said my husband, Tony, suddenly one day several years ago.

"What kind of animal is that?" I asked.

"It's a cat with spots as well as stripes and is a distant cousin of the tiger," Tony told me. At the word 'tiger', I began to feel anxious.

"How big are they?" I asked.

Tony assured me that the average ocelot is about the height and length of a slim, but muscular, spaniel and weighs between twenty-five and forty pounds, though some do grow up to sixty pounds. I asked which country they came from and Tony told me that ocelots are found in South America and as far north as Mexico. I did not like the idea of animals which were basically wild being kept in captivity, but Tony said that as the jungles and plains of the ocelots' natural habitat were rapidly being destroyed and as these cats were cruelly hunted for their attractive skins – fourteen ocelot skins are needed for a full-length fur coat – he would like to try to breed them to help prevent these beautiful creatures becoming extinct. Ultimately he would like to see the governments of the countries concerned establishing National Parks, like the African ones, for the ocelots and other wildlife. In that event, he hoped that his ocelots could be used to help stock these parks.

I asked if they could be tamed, my alarm increasing.

Tony replied that they are very easy to tame when young, especially if they are handled by humans when their eyes are still closed, and sometimes when they are adult too, depending, of course, on the temperament of the cat concerned.

History records that ocelots were kept as pets by the Mexican Aztecs and by the Incas too. I have seen a photograph of a pottery figure of a man from the ancient Mochica tribe in Peru who is carrying a pet ocelot on his shoulder, and in the Museo Larco Hoyle in Lima, Peru, there are several Mochica figurines of a tame ocelot-like cat sitting at the feet of a high official who is seated on a throne, which may have been made between 100 B.C. and A.D. 500.

Before we met and married, Tony had lived for ten years in South Africa, where he spent a considerable time in game reserves. He was born in England, went to school at Lancing College in Sussex and then took a degree in engineering. A couple of years after graduating, Tony accepted an executive position with a company in Johannesburg in South Africa, during the course of which he spent many months in the bush, where he gained valuable knowledge and experience in the care and handling of animals, particularly the cats. Although he had always had animals round him as a boy in England – the sick and the motherless young especially seemed to find him – his time in Africa was really the beginning of his life long concern, compassion and affinity for animals.

I agreed to help Tony to try to breed ocelots, never thinking for one moment that we would be able to obtain one ocelot, let alone two, as they were difficult to find being an endangered species. But I was to be proved wrong. The only animals I had kept as a child were domestic cats – the alley cat type rather than pedigree felines.

It so happens that the family dentist is near Harrods and always after our visit to him, and also at other times, Tony and I visit their Pet Department. We did this so frequently that the staff got to know us and in particular of Tony's experience with animals, especially cats, in Africa.

One day, Tony complained of toothache, which is rare for him, so I made a dental appointment for him and also for myself at the same time. I had to have an anaesthetic and as I staggered back into the waiting-room, feeling as if my legs and head were made of cotton wool, Tony said that he had a surprise for me. I hazily remember saying, "Oh God, what?" having had previous experiences of Tony's surprises. It seems that when I was in the dentist's chair, Tony had visited, as usual, Harrod's Pet Department where he had been told that they had a six-month-old male ocelot for sale. Instantly, Tony said that he would buy it.

The ocelot kit's name was Snoopy, so named because he was curious. Snoopy's first action, when he was brought to us in the manager's office, was to investigate me, ladder my new tights and then urinate on me. I have not been able to make up my mind since whether that was approval or disapproval. I was so adamant that I did not want Snoopy, still being a little woozy from the anaesthetic, that when Tony offered me a five pound note as a bribe, I refused it and threatened to give up my full-time job as a secretary if he bought Snoopy. Tony did not say anything. I then thought it better if I left the manager's office. I thought, as I left Harrods, if only Tony had not had toothache at this particular time, he would not have bought Snoopy. As he is such a rare animal, someone else would have been bound to purchase him. When I returned home, I was not really surprised to find Snoopy already there, installed in a spare room in the house, but I refused to see him that day as I was still a little upset by the morning's incident.

The next morning I was eventually persuaded to see Snoopy, who looked so appealing and defenceless that I gave him an old jumper of mine to snuggle into and some more milk. When he had finished drinking, he looked up at me with a soft expression in his big brown eyes and I immediately regretted that I had rejected him the day before. I sat down beside him to try to make friends with him and he came up to me slowly, sniffed my hands and licked me before curling up at my feet. I began, hesitantly at first, to stroke him and also to examine him as I did not have much opportunity to do so the previous day.

The background colouring on the top of his head and back was very rich amber, shading to white on his stomach, with white patches round his eyes and mouth. There was a large single white spot on the back of his jet-black ears, exactly the same as his distant cousin, the tiger. A black stripe ran upwards from the inner corner of each eye to his ears and another black stripe extended from the outer corner of each eye to the base of his ears. His stomach and feet were covered with spots and the stripes were mainly on his face, the top of his head and along his backbone. On his sides, there were horseshoe-shaped black markings round amber fur, in the centre of which was a single small black spot. He had the darker colouring of the jungle cat whereas ocelots from the plains, particularly from Mexico, have lighter coats. He was about the size of an average domestic cat, but with heavier bones and stronger muscles. I always shudder when I see a woman wearing an ocelot fur coat, knowing that fourteen ocelots are needed for a full-length coat and that very rarely are such cats killed humanely.

When I got up to leave, Snoopy became agitated and kept rubbing himself backwards and forwards against my feet. When I did manage to close the door on him, I heard him pacing to and fro and learnt afterwards that a cat always paces ceaselessly when unhappy.

Snoopy had been first bought several weeks before and placed in a small cage in a flat in Mayfair as a sort of living *objet d'art*. Naturally, being a young kit, he wanted to run around and play and when he was not allowed to do so, had started to nip and scratch. He was returned to Harrods as being vicious. On learning this, I gave Snoopy all the love and affection that I could, spending as much time with him as possible, playing continuously with him until, eventually, he did not mind being by himself when we had to go out. However, Tony told me that even though I might think Snoopy to be sweet and cuddly, he was still a jungle cat and that I must have a healthy respect for him as he could, if he so wished, inflict considerable injury depending on his temperament. I should not go in to him on my own until I had gained more experience in the handling of these animals, which I could only achieve slowly. Our relationship should be that of comrades. One cannot force one's will upon these cats.

Snoopy did not miaow like a domestic cat and rarely made any noise, but when he did, it was a deep-throated growl. His whiskers were indicative of his moods; when they were flat against his face he was happy and relaxed but when there was danger or he was unsure of anything or anyone, his whiskers would begin to come forward until they were pointing straight in front of him.

He was very clean and when I found that he used only one corner of the room as a toilet place, I put some newspaper on the floor there. I did give him a toilet tray once, but he thought this was a toy and kicked it all over the room. If Snoopy remained in the house when he became adult, I would have to arrange the newspaper in such a way as to form a backing as well because male ocelots spray urine. In the wild, this spraying would be to define the male's territory.

Snoopy was not vicious with us, but he did nip – sometimes hard. His nipping never drew blood nor did he use his claws on us and I was to read later that ocelots throughout their lives will always nip and cannot be stopped from doing this, as it is natural for them to nip each other in play.

Finding the correct toys for Snoopy was a problem; he could not have any toys made of plastic, soft rubber or similar materials or stuffed with pieces of foam rubber because if he swallowed these, they could become lodged in his stomach and cause death. Finally, both he and I settled on raw carrots and hard-boiled eggs. He especially liked to play with the eggs, when he would roll and kick them around like a football or else throw them up into the air until the shells cracked. He was very affectionate, not aloof as the domestic cat tends to be and we noticed that he rubbed his back feet on the ground in a shuffling or marking-time movement whenever anything gave him pleasure. Like his cousin, the tiger, Snoopy enjoyed water. When I gave him water instead of milk to drink, he would invariably put his paw into the bowl to play, flicking it around the room.

Tony bought Snoopy a collar and lead and took him around the garden to begin with but soon he was walking so well on the lead that we went further afield. The first time that he was taken into the country he was most intrigued with tall rough grass, unlike our lawn, and weeds. He sniffed them and suddenly snapped at a stinging nettle, biting it off from its stem. As the nettle stung his mouth, he sprang up into the air, like a vertical take-off aircraft. He saw two ponies in a paddock, jumped from Tony's arm on to the fence and sat quite still for several moments gazing at them. He was suspicious of cows and pulled Tony away from the path to the fence so that he could get a better view of them.

On another such walk, Snoopy saw a shallow stream and raced straight to it. For the next hour, he thoroughly enjoyed playing in the water, tapping it with his paws, jumping and trying to nip the resulting spray, rubbing his neck and shoulders along the stream's stony bed. When he had finished playing, I coaxed him into a clump of bracken and rolled him over and over to dry, making it into a game. Other people were also enjoying a pleasant walk in the woods with their dogs, and after Snoopy was dry, we continued our walk. Snoopy, who was tired by this time, was walking quietly on his lead when we met a group of people with unleashed dogs. The humans froze at the sight of Snoopy, but their dogs immediately ran up to him. He ignored them at first, but as he was still only a few months old and much smaller than the adult hounds, Tony picked him up out of their reach. Normally, Snoopy enjoyed playing with dogs, providing they were his own size. There is a Manchester terrier belonging to a neighbour with whom he often played.

On returning to our island home, we walked through the neglected and down-at-heel orchard outside our garden gate. The orchard is now taken over by nettles and other wild plants and, in summer, many varieties of butterfly flutter and dance in the sunlight. Snoopy saw a butterfly and immediately sprang to try to catch it, missed and landed in a bed of stinging nettles, his nose stung. Since then, he ignores the butterflies and also bumble bees by which he has also been stung when he became too curious.

Tony and I also have a domestic cat, which was our first animal. It is female, called Willy – short for Wilhelmenia, with fur like black velvet. We met Willy when we were renting a flat in Putney. She belonged to some other tenants upstairs who shortly before had bought a puppy, which constantly jumped on Willy, naturally wanting to play. By that time, Willy was about six years old and approaching a cat's middle-age. She had been neutered and had put on weight, especially round her stomach which hung down almost touching the ground. Willy was becoming sedate, and when we arrived she began to come into our flat for peace away from the puppy.

Willy became part of our lives. She came to us not only for a quiet place in which to sleep, but for affection and companionship as well. She would seek us out, then sit and watch us and when we spoke to her, she would rub herself against our legs, raising her face to us, purring deeply and loudly.

At that time, we owned a boat which was moored at the coast about eighty miles away and Tony and I went to it every weekend. On our return each Sunday night, we would find Willy sitting waiting for us by the garden gate. Another tenant told us that he would see Willy take up her position by the gate early on the Sunday afternoon and sit, motionless for hours, waiting for our return.

One day, we noticed that Willy was constantly scratching her left ear and shaking her head, which was indicative of an ear complaint. As she was not receiving treatment for this, Tony saw her owners, who were not concerned, so he surreptitiously took her to a vet. himself, who diagnosed an abscess and treated it successfully.

Just before we moved from the Putney flat to our house on an ait, a small island, in the Thames, our landlady, a cat lover, asked us if we would take Willy with us. She told us that when Willy's owners had gone away on a fortnight's holiday, they had left with her only four tins of cat food as being an adequate supply during their absence.

So, at our landlady's suggestion, we kidnapped Willy about a week before we were due to move and boarded her out in a cattery. We were not surprised when her owners showed no interest in her disappearance or concern for her safety.

Moving did not seem to worry Willy as long as she was with us, though we were anxious in case she fell into the River Thames. A few days later she was listless and refused food. Tony took her to a vet. who diagnosed that she was suffering from cat 'flu, caught at the cattery. He gave her injections and she recovered after a couple of weeks.

Our house on the ait is built on stilts with the river at the front of the island, a few yards from it. On some summer mornings, when the sky is azure without clouds, the rising sun shines on the mist enveloping the river creating a golden ethereal world which is soon shattered by the boats gliding past. At the rear of the island is the backwater leading to a lake called Tumbling Bay, where trout and otter have been seen occasionally. No cars are able to come to our part of the island, so all is peaceful and quiet except for the occasional high-pitched shout of the young coach urging the schoolboy rowers to do better.

I never feel isolated from life living by the river as there is usually some living being around, people walking on the opposite towpath, sometimes with children and dogs, their voices carrying clearly across the water, and boats travelling up or down stream, even in winter's blinding snowstorms. The majestic river steamers, now converted to jazz boats, plying the Thames at night from Easter to October, strung with hundreds of twinkling fairy lights, full of loud music and thumping feet. Numerous fishermen, sitting like statues along the banks, at dusk lighting their tiny lanterns to glow comfortingly through the night. The sleek river rats, so superior to their scruffy town cousins, running up the mooring lines of boats or along the banks. Mother ducks, in springtime, proudly leading flotillas of brown fluff until sometimes, very suddenly, a duckling disappears under water pulled down and eaten by a hungry pike. The sound of a female duck flying up to a window ledge to perch there waiting to be fed with her mate waiting on the lawn a few feet away. The heavy whirring beat of the swans' wings as they fly overhead, then sending up sprays of water as they skid along the surface before finally landing on the river. Above all, the feeling that the Thames is a route along which one can escape in a boat, upstream to Oxford or downstream to France.

Willy did fall into the Thames, but only on one occasion. It happened that someone had been cutting a lawn further up river and had thrown the grass cuttings into the water. These had floated downstream in a clump and wedged against our quay. Willy must have thought that this was solid ground because I saw her make an elegant leap on to the cuttings and slowly sink, a look of utter surprise on her face. I rushed forward, but was unable to reach her in time because just before her head went under, she managed to scramble up the bank to safety, with only her dignity injured. After that, it was many weeks before I saw Willy venture to the river's edge again,but when she did, it was to crouch down for a long time on the quay looking into the water. Suddenly, she put her paw into the river in a scooping movement and when I went to see what she was doing, I found her trying unsuccessfully to catch some of the hundreds of tiny fish which were milling around just below the surface.

A few days after Snoopy's arrival, Willy was taken into his room to be formally introduced. Tony placed her on a low table, whereupon Snoopy slowly walked up to her, sniffed and began purring and rubbing himself against the side of the table. He then put his face up to Willy, who gave him a couple of quick taps on the top of his head, in rebuke for coming too near her. Snoopy rolled over on his back, all four legs in the air, looked at her with his big brown eyes as if to say, 'What have I done to deserve this, I only want to be friends'.

As Snoopy grew older and became rough and boisterous, we kept Willy away from him as much as possible. Once, Willy did roll over, coquettishly, to show Snoopy her stomach, but he bounded over and nipped her playfully.

She struggled to her feet and hurried off, on her stiff legs, her stomach wobbling, her tail erect and quivering indignantly at the tip.

Tony built Snoopy a large daytime enclosure in the garden so that there was no danger of him falling into the Thames. As he had an extrovert nature and seemed to enjoy being taken out, Snoopy sometimes travelled in Tony's car to distant isolated woods. His favourite place in the car was on the floor in front of the passenger seat beside the driver, but when I sat there, my feet were in his way, so he began to nip them until I learnt, painfully, to sit with my feet drawn up to my chin. Once, when Snoopy was asleep on the back ledge of the car, Tony noticed a police car following us for mile after mile. Eventually, they stopped us to ascertain whether or not Snoopy was a stuffed toy! Tony invited the police officers to stroke him, but they declined.

On another occasion, the roads were so congested because of an accident that policemen were supervising the traffic flow. It was a hot summer's day and some of the officers had discarded their tunics and were working with their shirt sleeves rolled up. Tony's car was the first to be halted by such a constable, who turned his back on us to watch his colleagues elsewhere. Snoopy was sitting on the back seat and became most curious of the hairy, broad arm so near him with the fingers pointing straight at the side of the car. The driver's window was open and the cat, who by this time was no longer a kit but had grown rapidly, stood on the back of the front seat and stretched his head and neck out of the window and sniffed the tips of the officer's fingers. Tony was holding Snoopy's collar as a safety precaution. The constable must have felt him, but did not turn round as he was so engrossed in watching the other traffic and probably though it was a dog. The other motorists with us in the queue noticed and some began to grin and to nudge their passengers to watch. A distant policeman saw Snoopy and waved to his colleague to look round. He turned his head and when he saw the spotted and striped cat gazing up at him, his eyes widened momentarily in astonishment and disbelief. The seconds seemed long before suddenly he jerked his still outstretched arm away and hurriedly walked off with raised arm to the other lane of traffic before returning to wave us on and away.

A favourite ocelot game is 'touch', which Snoopy enjoyed. It happened that one day, Snoopy, whom I thought was asleep on the back ledge of the car, suddenly jumped on me from behind and put his paws over my eyes. I immediately thought that he could tear my eyes out, but all he wanted was for me to play with him. We taught him never to touch Tony whilst he was driving the car and so, eventually, he would either curl up on Tony's lap or on the floor and go to sleep.

As Snoopy was so reliable with humans, he occasionally modelled and one of his first modelling assignments was to pose on a newly developed upholstery material which the manufacturers claimed was scratch-proof. A chair in a pub had been specially upholstered with this new fabric and Tony was told to take the cat there.

Snoopy behaved well, sitting on the chair elegantly, surrounded by young and glamorous girls, the two photographers moving around him for what seemed to be long hours until finally he became bored. He yawned, spreading and stretching his front paws, his claws unsheathed and languidly ripped the supposedly scratch-proof upholstery material right across the seat of the chair. The publicity man looked horrified, the photographic session was thrown into confusion and Tony and Snoopy departed as there was no point in staying any longer with non-scratch material.

Another modelling job was with Cliff Richard, the singer. Snoopy was nervous of the studio and bright lights and was reluctant at first to pose. Cliff was extremely concerned for his welfare and waited patiently for him to become more relaxed until eventually their photograph was taken together. Both Tony and I will never forget Cliff's kindness and consideration for Snoopy.

Snoopy also appeared on *Magpie*, the children's television programme, but again disliked the studio atmosphere and bright lights and stayed in his box. He was eventually coaxed out, but immediately made a horrid smelling 'mess' on the studio floor, much to the natural disgust of the studio hands who had to dispose of it. However, he made amends by assisting with the publicity for *Magpies* sixpence collection for the United Nations International Children's Emergency Fund, the purpose of which was to equip a new medical centre for a community in the Paraguayan jungle. Snoopy's photograph was taken holding in his mouth one of the donation cheques, which embarrassingly, he chewed into pieces!

Snoopy became the official mascot of H.M.S. *Ocelot*, a submarine, and Tony was requested to take him to Portsmouth so that he could be presented to his ship. An admiral's barge collected us at the quay side and took us to the waiting submarine. I shivered a little as I saw the submarine and thought how ominous it looked. Its black paint, with no other colour as relief, made it appear most sinister.

Snoopy posed for the photographers quite happily on what seemed to me to be a tiny deck, though he appeared a little nervous of the Captain. We think this was because the skipper was wearing gloves; Snoopy would always immediately pull them off my hands and tear them to pieces – perhaps he did not dare to do this to the Captain!

Some of the ship's crew were asked to pose with their mascot and formed a semi-circle round Snoopy, who kept looking nervously at one sailor in particular. We could not think why until we looked at the photographs later. All the other sailors had either folded their arms or put their hands into their pockets, but this one sailor had clasped his hands together in front of him so that they were, inadvertently, pointing directly at Snoopy, who naturally wondered if this was an act of aggression.

After this photographic session, Tony was presented with a bronze plaque bearing the name H.M.S. *Ocelot*, showing an ocelot rising from the sea whose raised paw is covered with blood, claws unsheathed, in a striking position.

In H.M.S. *Ocelot*'s minute wardroom, we were interested to see a stuffed ocelot in a glass case. This ocelot's colouring was different from Snoopy's, being much paler indicating that it was a cat from the sandy plains.

While Snoopy was being photographed inside the submarine, sitting on Tony's lap, surrounded by the crew and their wives and children, someone closed a door with a crash, startling him. He swung round and jumped up, unintentionally hooking his claws into Tony's lip, pulling it down. Tony could do nothing to help himself as he did not want to let go of Snoopy as he had visions of him disappearing inside the sub. amongst its intricate machinery, so I had to gently clasp Snoopy's paw and unhook it from Tony's lip. After that, we decided that Snoopy had had enough and we left.

Some months later, Tony was asked if Snoopy would appear in a television programme about the skins from animals being used for fur coats. A member of the public brought a gin trap to the studio to illustrate how cruelly some animals are caught and to balance the programme a well-known furrier also took part. Snoopy sat on Tony's lap to show that his coat looked better on him than made up into a garment for a human. It was during this discussion that the furrier confirmed that the skins from fourteen ocelots are needed for a full-length fur coat.

A bank account was opened especially for Snoopy's fees from modelling called *Snoopy Ocelot Enterprises* to pay for his food and vet.'s bills, but when he continued to appear unhappy in photographic studios, Tony removed his name from the books of animal employment agencies.

Chapter Two

As Snoopy grew older, Tony and I began thinking about a mate for him and wondered if there was a female ocelot in Britain which might be suitable. We made enquiries at various zoos and visited a zoological supplier but none had an ocelot, neither male nor female, and were not hopeful of being able to obtain one domestic born as these cats are so scarce. We did not want to be responsible for an ocelot being taken from the jungle because the statistics are that for every ten ocelots shipped from Central and South America, seven or eight will die *en route*. If an ocelot kit is desired, the mother usually has to be killed first because she is so protective of her young.

On our way out from the zoological suppliers, we looked into some of the animal cages. One cage contained several eagle owls and in the corner, all by itself and looking most dejected, was another kind of owl. The man in charge, Reg Matta, who, we were to find out later, is very expert and knowledgeable regarding animals, told us that this was a Malayan Fish Owl, which his three children had christened Fred. The eagle owls had ganged up on Fred, taking all the food so that he had to be fed by hand, consequently he had become very tame and friendly to humans.

Reg lifted Fred off the perch and brought him over to us. I put my hand in front of his feet, but Reg told me that as birds of prey step backwards, I should place my hand behind Fred to take him on to me. I looked at his talons on my hand and thought how sharp they looked but was surprised to find my hand unscathed. Fred's beak was large and hooked, so I put my index finger, very slowly, up to his beak to see if he would peck me and if so, how viciously.

He looked down at my fingers and very gently nibbled them, then he moved along my arm until his body was pressing into me. After several minutes, Reg took him and stroked and blew softly into his chest feathers. I asked Reg whether Fred hooted like English owls, but was told that the only sounds which he made were very low pitched, whistling noises and also a rapid clicking noise when he was angry.

When Reg placed him back in the cage with the eagle owls, Fred made an angry clicking sound. The four eagle owls looked at him and then started moving towards him. He shuffled into a corner, but the eagle owls still advanced and one began to spread its wings to fly at him. Tony and I felt sorry for the solitary Malayan fish owl and as he had been so gentle with me, we decided to buy him. Reg entered the cage, the eagle owls were still looking aggressive, picked Fred up and placed him on Tony's arm. Tony stroked his head gently, Fred whistled hoarsely, preened himself, and nestled down.

On the way home in the car, Fred sat on the back of my passenger seat. Reg had told us that as Malayan fish owls sit motionless for hours in their natural habitat, Fred would sit quite happily on my seat without trying to fly around inside the car. Reg was right, the only movement which Fred made on the journey home was to move his head up and down in a bobbing movement whenever he saw something which interested him, much to the surprise of the other motorists, especially when we stopped at traffic lights. He was also interested in my long hair and kept picking it up and running it through his beak. I turned round to talk to him, but found that his head had 'disappeared'; he had twisted it almost right the way round to his back to look at a car coming up fast behind us. Later in the journey, he started to make a coughing sound, then he regurgitated a small pellet of feathers. I was anxious, but Tony told me that it was perfectly natural for Fred to do this once a day. If he did not, he would die as this pellet was the result of all the bones and feathers which his body could not absorb.

Fred was about eighteen inches high, his eyes the colour of buttercups with long eye lashes; the feathers on his chest were light chocolate brown, tipped with black, and the feathers on his back were a much darker brown, with pale buff-coloured 'bars' every couple of inches. His ears were long and pointed and above his beak was a triangular band of cream feathers.

I tried to find more information on Malayan fish owls, but there is hardly any except that they are semi-nocturnal, being mostly active at dusk. They frequent rice fields, streams, lakes and the coastal waters of the Malayan Peninsula. Their main diet, in the wild, consists of frogs, crustaceans, fish, water-bugs and insects, but in captivity they will accept small mammals and day-old dead chicks. The sexes are alike, with the female being sometimes bigger than the male and apart from that there is no other indication, so we had no idea whether Fred was male or female.

I bought many different kinds of fish for Fred, together with shell fish, but he would not eat any of them. At first, I gave him small pieces of meat rolled up in feathers from an old pillow case for roughage, which he ate until someone suggested dead turkey or chicken poults, which have been the basis of his diet ever since.

I placed several washing-up bowls filled with water in Fred's aviary, so that he could paddle. Frequently, I saw him hop on to a bowl's rim, perch there for several moments staring down into the water before jumping down into it to bathe himself, flapping his wings and shaking the long feathers on his legs, which look like trousers.

Whenever Fred saw one of us, he would give his hoarse, whistling noise, which sounds like slowly escaping steam, which he has continued to do to this day, especially when he hears my voice. If we go across to talk to him, he hops off his perch and stands just behind the door waiting to be picked up. If Tony or I do not have the time for him, he goes to the window and stands, bobbing up and down, watching us.

Our visitors are taken to see Fred and he will perch happily on anyone's arm to be stroked and petted. He likes especially to have his head scratched just behind his ear. He seems to be fascinated by hair, particularly by long female hair and also by men with beards, into which he rubs his beak. A bald man, without a beard, was once taken to see Fred, who perched on his arm, bobbing up and down and looking quizzically at him all the time. Even when I placed Fred on another visitor's arm, he ignored her and kept looking at the shining bald head.

All this time, Tony was still trying to obtain a mate for Snoopy and we wondered if there might be a female ocelot kept privately in Britain whose owner would be willing to mate with our male. We inserted the following advertisement in the Personal Column of *The Times*: "Mate wanted for Snoopy ocelot. Fertile females (ocelots only!)"

But again we were unsuccessful. Tony then applied for a licence, which was granted, to import a domestically born female ocelot from the United States.

At the end of March, with only a limited period in which to find a female ocelot and have her imported to England, we had to act rapidly. The next day, Tony called at the American Embassy in London and explained the urgency of his quest. The Americans were very helpful and immediately assigned a secretary to assist Tony in drawing up a list of possible ocelot suppliers.

We wrote about a dozen letters, all with pre-paid replies, and sent them off to the United States. Then we heard that there was a postal strike in New York, which lost five days from our precious thirty. Tony then resorted to telephoning and called two firms in Miami, four in New York, all with negative replies. He also cabled another six suppliers saying: "Can you supply a female unaltered ocelot, up to two years old, must arrive England by 19th April."

This allowed us fourteen days' emergency grace if it were needed.

The first reply was negative; another could not guarantee live delivery; then Dr. Wallach from Brookfield Zoo cabled: "We do not have any ocelots in the collection at this time, sorry cannot supply."

Tony telephoned another number in the United States and was, by error, put through to a swimming pool. We read a newspaper story about a vagrant clown who was deemed in need of care and attention in California with a caravan full of animals – monkeys, bears, birds and an ocelot, but we could not trace him. Then a cable arrived from Everglades Pet Shop saying: "Cannot help you, but try Upsetexchange 2881 Fulton Street, Brooklyn, New York."

'Upsetexchange' did not sound like a pet shop, but the cable was clear enough. So we sent another cable, but fortunately the U.S. mail men realised that two letters had been transposed and delivered our cable correctly to the U.S. Pet Exchange.

The owner, Ray Webber, replied saying that he could supply a female ocelot, costing four hundred dollars. Tony hurried to the bank and arranged for the money to be sent over. Ray Webber then telephoned to say that there was an airline strike, but he would try to enlist the aid of the

British Consul; also, he had not received the money. Again Tony went to the bank, who on investigation found that our dollars had been 'lost' *en route* and so replacement money was dispatched. Earlier, he had telephoned the British overseas telephone operators to try to ascertain the telephone number for 'Upsetexchange' and on being initially unsuccessful, had sent a cable. At eight o'clock on Easter Sunday morning, a telephone operator from the overseas exchange rang to say that they had managed to sort out 'Upsetexchange' into U.S. Pet Exchange, she had the telephone number and had we received the cable which Ray Webber had sent the previous day? We had not, and spent the next two hours trying to locate it. It transpired that as we do not have a telegraphic address, this one vital cable had been returned by our local office as being unknown. Tony had given our telephone number after our address and by this method, all the unimportant cables, and also Ray Webber's first cable, had reached us safely. Eventually it was traced and read: "Will ship Monday 10 p.m. Flight 506 BOAC", which would arrive in England on the Tuesday morning.

We arrived at London Airport early to await the arrival of our female ocelot. By 11.30 a.m. there was no news; the plane had arrived on schedule but apparently there was no sign of an ocelot. At last at two o'clock in the afternoon we were told that she had landed on the 10.40 a.m. plane, but that all the plane's documents had been left in New York, hence the delay. By this time, we were very worried about her condition after the transatlantic flight and whether she had enough food and water. We hurried to the R.S.P.C.A. Airport Hostel to see if she was there, and if not, to enlist their help to check her condition. We asked to see the hostel manager, Neville Whittaker, who was very helpful. He said that they did not have our ocelot there but that he would come with us straight away to check on her.

On the way back to the Cargo Centre I said to Mr. Whittaker that it was fortunate she had arrived during the day when the R.S.P.C.A. could attend to her. Mr. Whittaker told me that it would not have made any difference if she had arrived at night as the R.S.P.C.A. hostel is open twenty-four hours – the girls staff it at night as well, though he, or his male deputy, attend to any animals which are considered to be dangerous. Tony asked if our ocelot could be kept at the R.S.P.C.A. hostel until she was fit enough to travel to the quarantine centre as we had no idea of her condition and she might be suffering from the effects of the long flight. Neville Whittaker readily agreed as the hostel is equipped with its own quarantine quarters. In fact, they had recently cared for three adult cheetahs which had arrived in a collapsed state. They were given intensive care, including drip feeds, and one cheetah was in such bad condition that it was on the drip feed for seven days. Although the R.S.P.C.A. has only a temporary quarantine station at the airport, they were given special permission by the Ministry of Agriculture and the cheetahs were detained for a further three weeks while they recuperated.

Neville Whittaker also told us about a baby gorilla which arrived at the hostel on its way to the United States. It was only a few months old and was too ill to continue the journey. It was given intensive care and it was in a cradle in a corner of the office for many weeks. It wore nappies and eventually was trained to use a chamber pot, though its head had to be held whilst it was sitting on the pot.

When animals arrive dead, it is in the majority of cases the crates which are the culprits. Some years ago several hyenas had arrived at the hostel in tin boxes, and their only air supply was from old nail holes. At least one animal from every species that is transported arrives dead at some time.

The animals do not often escape on an aircraft but once,

a tiger, about three-quarters grown, managed to escape from its crate. Neville Whittaker and his deputy were called and found that the tiger had gone to the tail of the aircraft. It was, understandably, spitting and snarling so they got inside an empty crate and shuffled it forwards towards the tiger until they were able to inject it with a tranquilliser through an opening.

Mr. Whittaker told us that although the animals became considerably tame whilst at the R.S.P.C.A. hostel they do cause some difficulties at first. There was once a slight problem feeding one baby elephant. It so happened that the door to its enclosure opened inwards and when feeding time arrived the baby elephant pressed its foot against the door so that there was great difficulty in opening it. Elephants, particularly the baby ones, usually arrive very thirsty and drink gallons of milk during their stay at the hostel. One young elephant ate but would not drink and eventually the vet. advised giving it salt on its tongue thus succeeding in making it drink.

We arrived at the Cargo Centre, and Mr. Whittaker, who had been given permission by the airline, went to inspect our ocelot. He returned to report that she was alive and appeared to be very healthy and that she had plenty of food and drink left in the canisters which were attached to her cage. He told us that we need not have worried; the pet shop in New York had packed her very well in an adequate sized cage, which was covered with cardboard in which there were plenty of air holes. We thanked him for being so concerned and continued to wait for our animal.

At last, just before four o'clock, our female ocelot was released by B.O.A.C. and Tony went to see her and found that part of the cardboard covering had been torn off. His first glimpse of her was of two big eyes and a pink nose looking out through the tear. Written on the cardboard wrapping was: 'Live animal. Do not expose to extreme heat or cold'; 'Please keep in warm place'; 'Do not tease'; 'This side up'; and 'Please check food and water'.

During the day we had met a *Daily Express* photographer whom we knew and he took a photograph of the ocelot looking out through the bars of her cage.

"What's her name?" he asked.

We did not know and so on the spur of the moment Tony said, "Sheba".

Sheba's colouring was much paler than Snoopy's, indicating that she is a cat from sandy plains. Her bone structure was not good and her front legs were bowed, indicating a lack of vitamins when she was a kit. And so Sheba went into quarantine for nine months.

A few days later, Tony received a telegram from an Englishman who had seen Sheba's photograph and story in the *Daily Express*, to say that he owned a female ocelot. He had been on holiday in Mexico some weeks earlier and had purchased an ocelot there. This ocelot had been owned by people who bred parrots and as she continuously chased the birds had to be sold. He brought the ocelot back to England and Tony arranged to go with him to see her three days later. Before they could do so she died.

About a month after Sheba's entry into quarantine, it was noticed that she had put on weight. She was examined by three vets. all of whom confirmed that she was pregnant. We knew that she had been kept with other ocelots in America, but we never thought that we would be so lucky as to buy a pregnant cat. She produced milk, and grew fatter. We waited and waited until after the ninety days' gestation period, assuming that she had mated just before leaving America. She did not give birth. A Ministry of Agriculture vet. was called in and his verdict was that Sheba had a genuine 'phantom' pregnancy.

We travelled to the quarantine centre every weekend, though only Tony was allowed to see Sheba while I waited outside. At first, she would not allow Tony near her, but after a very short time became friendly and sucked Tony's jacket, leaving wet patches, in which Snoopy was most interested when we arrived home! Tony told me that he always felt extremely sad at the end of his visit when the quarantine door was closed and Sheba was left alone because he knew that she craved human company and affection.

During Sheba's quarantine life continued smoothly at home. Snoopy was taken for walks regularly and as Fred Owl was an extrovert and liked human companionship, Tony and I often had him in the house when visitors called. At these times, of course, Snoopy was 'banished' to his outdoor enclosure. Tony made a perch especially for Fred and I placed newspaper underneath as it was impossible to house train him.

One of Fred's favourite perches was in an old apple tree where he attracted the attention of other birds, which used to mob him, especially the starlings, but he just gazed at them unblinkingly and twisted his head almost right the way round to his back to follow their progress as they hopped round him. After a short time, they became used to him and would come up to within inches of him.

One day, I was watching a comedy show on television and thought what a splendid stooge Fred would make for a comedian as he would perch without moving on anybody's arm, except for his head looking round when spoken to. I mentioned this idea to Tony who thought that I should write to some television companies suggesting this and enclosing a photograph of Fred.

One of the scriptwriters I wrote to passed my letter on to a children's programmes producer who, coincidentally, was looking for a bird to act as a pet of one of the characters in a new series. It was arranged that the producer and director, as they both lived near us, would visit us for Fred's preliminary 'audition' in our garden.

There is an ancient and disused pump to a well in the garden, which was one of Fred's favourite perches as from there he could see into the overgrown orchard outside the garden gate to watch the butterflies amongst the nettles or in the other direction, watch the River Thames with its variety of boats. On sighting the producer and director entering the garden gate, Fred bobbed up and down, moving his head from side to side, peering at them. Tony placed the owl on the producer's arm, Fred wobbled and then regained his balance, and whistling hoarsely was carried round the garden. The director wondered how tame he was and lifted Fred on his arm to his hair. Fred, as usual, was interested in hair and gently nibbled the director's dark curly locks. The producer and director left saying that they had a toucan to see as well for the part and would let us know. A few days later, a letter arrived to say that Fred had been chosen as Ozymandius in *The Ace of Wands*.

Tony, Fred and I arrived at the television studios to find that a special perch had been made for Fred on a set depicting an artist's studio. He sat on his perch, without moving, and whilst filming was in progress on other sets, went to sleep while his set was in semi-darkness. When the lights and cameras were turned on him, he was instantly awake and, after a time, seemed to realise what it was all about and that the cameras pointing at him meant that he was the centre of attention.

Fred formed an attachment for one of the cameramen and regularly flew on to the top of his camera, and hopped along the top of it to stand gazing at him. Then we realised that this particular cameraman had a beard and it was this that was fascinating to the owl. He would sometimes gate-crash a scene and fly on to an actor's shoulder. This was so natural that it was retained. During the filming of the last few episodes, Fred became cocky and began joining in, by whistling, whenever the actors spoke their lines. An instruction came down from the producer's box to the floor manager to remove the bird to a dark corner out of earshot. Fred looked most forlorn and dejected away from the action and kept very silent.

During the next day's filming, a snake was used on another set in the studio. Fred saw it moving, gazed intently at it for many minutes and then prepared to fly over to inspect a possible source of food, as these owls will kill snakes in the wild. We quickly shut him away but from then on, when he was returned to his perch after the snake had gone, he kept peering at the spot where it had been. If he saw a thick television cable on the studio floor, he would make a sudden dive onto it, presumably thinking it was a snake, much to the consternation of the director.

Afterwards, Tony said that the snake was exactly like Monty, a reptile he had known whilst living in Johannesburg. At that time, he rented a room from the family McDonald, who kept chickens. The only store for the chickens' grain was the garage, which soon became infested with rats and mice. They thrived on the chickens' food and the domestic cat was unsuccessful in catching them.

On his next trip to Durban, Tony went to the Fitzsimmons Snake Park and, whilst there, purchased a snake as a rat and mouse catcher, which he christened Monty. On the return journey to Johannesburg, with two friends, Tony, who was driving the car, placed Monty in a box on the floor beside him. During the journey, the snake forced open the lid of the box, slithered out, climbed up Tony's trouser leg and around his waist for warmth and then, after a little while, emerged from his collar. Immediately, there was a shriek from the friend sitting in the back of the car. Tony slammed on the brakes, nearly skidding into a ditch, and turned round to see what was wrong. He found his friend sitting with his knees drawn up to his chin, his face ashen, his eyes bulging as he was petrified of snakes.

Monty was a very successful rat catcher and grew fat. He became a pet of the McDonald children, but not of the cleaning lady. One day, he escaped from the garage, slithered unseen into the house and eventually curled round a tall lamp standard and went to sleep. The cleaning lady arrived and because Monty was nearly the same colour as the lamp standard and as she was a little short-sighted, she did not notice him. She dusted the lamp and Monty vigorously, until he moved, his sleep disturbed, and began to slither away. There was a loud scream, then a thud and silence as the cleaning lady fainted onto the carpet.

Monty continued to live for some years until, one day, he tried to crawl up the huge exhaust pipe of Mrs. McDonald's car. He had grown too fat, became stuck and suffocated.

As we have always disliked keeping a single wild creature in captivity without the companionship of its own kind, we applied for a permit to import two more Malayan fish owls, which was granted. Three owls arrived however, the third was a youngster, still with its baby down, fluffy feathers, squawking noisily and with Fred Owl's extrovert curiosity towards man. The other two owls were timid adults, one with a large ring round its leg. The colony has settled in well together and we hope that they will breed.

Chapter Three

Snoopy was ill, passing and vomiting blood. He had kept inside his sleeping quarters for most of the morning, which was unusual for him, and by mid-afternoon had begun to pass excrement in which was granulated blood. He then began to retch continuously and eventually to vomit. The vomit was streaked with blood. Tony gently placed him in a carrying box and we took him to a vet.'s surgery, not our present marvellous vet. We had taken samples of Snoopy's vomit and urine and the vet. sent them away for analysis and told us that he suspected that Snoopy had been poisoned; his vomit contained pieces of stomach lining. He was not very hopeful of Snoopy recovering and said that all he could do was to give him an injection and if he survived the night, he might have a chance of living.

That night, Snoopy had a second haemorrhage and was losing strength rapidly. We took him into bed with us and Snoopy lay with his head wedged under Tony's armpit. We hardly slept but kept watch on the animal. During the night, Snoopy had a nightmare and was twitching so violently that Tony woke him. Instantly he sunk his teeth into Tony's armpit and hung on for what seemed ages. Tony spoke softly to him and he seemed to realise where he was and withdrew his teeth. He then licked the wounds he had inflicted. Tony had not stopped Snoopy biting him as he did not know how conscious the cat was and did not wish to risk him becoming more violent.

The following morning, Snoopy was worse and still passing and vomiting blood. He could not stand up and I held his hindquarters above newspaper while he urinated. He had only drunk a little water with glucose and unless an additional treatment were given he would die. Although the vet. had said that there was nothing more he could do, Tony remembered the experience that he had gained in Africa and obtained a coagulate which he injected into Snoopy once. During the evening, he haemorrhaged again, but this time it was not so massive and as he was still very weak we wrapped him in a towel and took him back into bed.

Towards morning, Snoopy cried plaintively and attempted to struggle out of bed. At this stage, Tony thought he was dying and woke me but instead, whilst being supported, Snoopy passed a pink motion. The haemorrhage had stopped. We mixed kaopectate and glucose in milk which Snoopy drunk and that morning, although still weak and unable to walk, he did not haemorrhage again and there were signs of slight improvement. I filled an aluminium hot water bottle, wrapped it in a towel and placed it beside him. Every two hours, he managed to drink more milk mixed with kaopectate and glucose and ate some pieces of chicken and rabbit which I had deboned and passed through the liquidiser.

The laboratory report on Snoopy's urine and vomit stated that they had contained traces of either slug pellet or arsenical weed killer but he gradually recovered, although it was three months before he was completely fit, and since then, has become more affectionate than ever.

While Snoopy was so ill, Tony was unable to visit Sheba, but when he did she recognised him and allowed him to pet her more than usual. For her size, Sheba was the noisiest cat in the quarantine quarters. Her cries were more frequent than those of the lions, tigers and leopards there. She always yowled when spoken to and thereafter would continue 'muttering' for several minutes. Usually she made a gurgling noise when she ate and when drinking would make 'yummy, yummy, yummy' sounds.

One day, Tony met me from work and presented me with a green feather, which was tipped with red and said that there were plenty more where that came from. I asked him what he meant but he just told me to wait until we reached home. At home, I saw a parrot in its cage, half covered with a cloth. Tony put his finger inside the cage and scratched the bird underneath its beak and the parrot rotated its head so that he could scratch a different part of it. Apparently Tony had met some people who were emigrating and on hearing of his love for animals, had asked him to take their parrot which they were leaving behind. The parrot's name was Handsome and his vocabulary consisted of only one word, 'Hullo', which he pronounced in a variety of tones.

Tony took Handsome out of his cage, and the little bird hopped on to my shoulder and gently tweaked my ear. I said "Hullo", but the bird remained silent merely cocking its head on one side and watching me with bright eyes. Tony had bought a supply of parrot seed and told me that as well, Handsome liked pieces of orange, cabbage leaves and celery. Soon after, Handsome developed a taste for porridge which he took from Tony's mouth! He soon began to recognise the porridge bowls and directly he saw them, he would fly on to Tony's shoulder to wait for his share. He also became fond of tea, but would become impatient waiting for it and would try to pull the cup away from Tony's mouth.

Handsome's addiction to tea reminded Tony of a turtle dove which he once had in Africa. He had found the tiny fledgling upon some concrete steps. It was so young that it was still all pink with no feathers and little down. He picked it up, found it to be alive and took the bird home. He made little balls of hard-boiled egg yolk and brown bread, impaled these on matchsticks, opened the fledgling's beak and gently pushed the food inside. The bird, which he named Tweety, greedily gulped them and ate as many as he was given.

Tweety grew into a beautiful turtle dove and was completely tame. He was free to fly away if he wished, but he did not and sat on Tony's shoulder almost everywhere he went. When the bird did not go out with him a window was left open so that he could fly freely in and out. Sometimes at night, Tweety would nestle in Tony's hair before flying on to the headboard of the bed which was the bird's sleeping place.

Tony had a habit of always drinking a cup of tea, laced with brandy, before going to bed. One evening, he spilt some of the brandy-laced tea into the saucer accidentally and Tweety flew on to the table and started drinking it. From then on, Tweety became addicted and began to recognise the teapot. Often, he would fly down to perch on the edge of the cup waiting for the tea to be poured out into it and then into the saucer.

One night, Tony accidentally poured more brandy than usual into the tea. He did not realise this until he saw that Tweety was drunk and having difficulty in reaching his sleeping place. Tony tried to help him, but Tweety kept tripping over his own feet chirruping merrily all the time. Eventually he flopped on to the carpet, where Tony left him as being the safest place to 'sleep it off'.

Whilst waiting for Tony to finish visiting Sheba, I stayed outside the quarantine section and, in doing so, began to know the manager, Cornishman Reg Matta and his wife Pam with their three young children, Julie, Louise and

Ruth. These children were each born in different zoos in Cornwall and Devon and had been exposed to animals from their first week.

Pam fed nearly one hundred animals daily, each with a different diet, and kept a supply of serum in her refrigerator. Part of her job was to hand feed abandoned animals such as tiger cubs and suckling monkeys. She told me that on one occasion a female gorilla had fallen in love with her husband and tried to drag him into her cage!

Once, Reg had been accidentally locked in a cage with a fully grown male African olive baboon, so called because of its greyish green colouring, which was about the size of an adult Alsatian dog. As the baboon was immensely strong, with canines nearly two inches long, he could have been badly injured if the animal had become aggressive, especially towards another male. Reg called for help, but all was silent, except for the various noises of the animals, as Pam and their assistant Peter were busy elsewhere. Reg kept cool and nonchalantly sat down on the floor. There was a large bunch of bananas in the cage so he took one and casually began to eat it. The baboon looked at him for a moment and then sat on the ground beside him, took another banana and began eating too. It then put its arm round Reg's shoulders in friendship, and they sat munching more bananas together.

After a while, Pam missed her husband and began to look for him. She was startled to find him sitting on the ground with the baboon, surrounded by banana skins.

"Why don't you join us for bananas," said Reg, jokingly, waving an arm airily in welcome. Pam vehemently declined and quickly unlocked the cage door. As the baboon was still engrossed in the bananas, Reg was able to extricate himself from the animal's embrace and quietly leave.

The three Matta children had been brought up never to be frightened of any of the animals but to have a healthy respect for them. They were taught never to stick their fingers in cages and not to run whilst in the zoo and thus frighten the animals. Julie, the eldest girl then aged seven, liked snakes and one day while I was there, picked one up and put it round her neck. I had always imagined snakes to be cold and slimy but when I touched it whilst it was round Julie's neck, I found it to be warm and dry.

On the way home, I told Tony about Julie and the snake and he said that normally snakes will not harm a human unless you are aggressive, like treading on them. He went on to tell me that he had trodden on a snake once, with almost fatal results.

When he was living in South Africa, he went to Happy Valley, a pleasure resort just outside Port Elizabeth. The sea is on one side of the road and a cafe and a park on the other, the far end of the park having been left in its wild state. He had gone to Happy Valley to try to photograph some monkeys and came across a female still carrying her baby. The monkey ran into the wild section of the park, Tony followed, but before he could photograph her, he felt, suddenly, an agonising pain in his leg, which felt as if molten metal had been injected into him. He heard a hiss, looked down and saw that he had trodden on a very poisonous yellow cobra. The snake reared its head to strike again, Tony jumped away and the cobra slithered off into the undergrowth. There was no one around as not many people ventured into the wild section and Tony knew that to remain alive after a yellow cobra's poisonous bite, a healthy male must have serum within a maximum of twenty minutes, depending on the amount of venom in the body and the person's physical condition. As he had no serum with him, he instinctively plunged his sheath-knife into the two puncture marks made by the cobra's fangs in his leg. He knew that he must bleed out as much of the poison as he could before attempting to reach the cafe and then on by car to the hospital.

Tony felt no pain from the knife, but he could not put a tourniquet on his leg as that would have impeded his running to the cafe. He did not know how much poison had been bled out and what amount was still left in his body. He ran as fast as he could, his foot squelching in the blood flowing down his leg and into his shoe. The cafe was at least half a mile away and he does not remember how long it took him to reach it. When he did arrive at the cafe, he felt as if every tooth was being slowly extracted without anaesthetic and there were tight bands round his head and chest. He remembers that he had acute difficulty in breathing.

He was pushed into a car and the cafe proprietor drove him to the hospital in about eight minutes. By the time he reached the Casualty Department, he felt no pain and just wanted to sleep. A doctor approached carrying a huge hypodermic syringe. Tony refused the injection and said that if only he were allowed to rest, he would be all right. He remembers vividly the feeling of numbness extending down the full length of his legs and a tingling sensation down his arms to the back of his hands. There followed a sensation of floating and of hardly breathing. Two nurses appeared, one on either side, slapping his face with the ends of wet towels and a third nurse poured scalding black coffee through his lips. The doctor told him that unless he had the injection he would die. He felt very drowsy, just wanting to sleep and still refused the injection. A few minutes later he went into a coma.

Tony was told later that while he was still conscious, one of the hospital staff had raced, by car, to the Magistrates Court to try to obtain a court order for him to be forcibly injected with the serum. This had not been granted, but once he became unconscious, the doctors were then able to inject the serum into him and thus save his life. Today, many years later, the scars from those sheath-knife cuts are still visible on his leg and each measures about an inch long by a quarter of an inch wide.

At last, Sheba's quarantine period was over and we went to collect her, taking Snoopy with us to meet his prospective mate. At the appointed hour, the large, solid zinc-lined door of the quarantine quarters was opened, then Sheba's cage door, but she did not move. Reg Matta called her several times but she remained still. She was not to know that now she was free and no longer in quanrantine. She was shown the choice pieces of meat which we had brought specially for her and gradually she was persuaded to move out of the quarantine section. Sheba was still wearing the collar, once bright red, now old and tattered, which she had worn on arrival from the United States. Tony attached a lead to it, gave a gentle tug and she trotted along, obviously used to going for walks. I was waiting with Snoopy on a lead, at the end of a corridor.

Sheba saw Snoopy and stopped, one front leg raised, whiskers forward, looking at him. Snoopy had never seen another ocelot before, except possibly his mother. His rear legs stiffened, his back arched slightly, his tail pointed straight up in the air and his whiskers were at right angles to his face, indicating that he was on the alert. He walked slowly towards Sheba, his legs stiff, stopped a few paces from her and sniffed the air. Sheba's whiskers were still forward and we expected a fight. She watched Snoopy. Tentatively, he edged nearer to her, then stretched his neck forward so that he could sniff her. They were nose to nose for a few moments, then Sheba put her paw down, her whiskers were flat against her face and she looked away and into the distance ignoring him. Snoopy backed, so I picked him up and placed him into a carrying case and into my ancient Ford Popular car. I have found out since that these exotic cats will not mate with just any of their kind, but have definite likes and dislikes.

Tony took Sheba in his car and told me that she was very quiet on the journey back until they were almost home when he, yet again, spoke to her and this time she answered with a soft yowl. He slowly put his fingers through the wire front of her carrying box and it was a wonderful moment when she rubbed herself against him.

Whilst Sheba was in quarantine, Tony had built a large run and sleeping quarters for the two ocelots. The sleeping quarters had a centre partition, which was removable if the cats were compatible. There was a small grille in this centre partition so that if we did have to separate them, the cats could still see each other. Without this grille, we thought that Sheba, especially, might be disturbed by the sound of an unknown animal on the other side.

When we arrived home, we put Sheba into the run, leaving Snoopy in his box temporarily, so that she could explore her new surroundings undisturbed. She sniffed around the compound and then ran into one section and jumped on to the shelf. We then put Snoopy into the run, but Sheba would not let him come near her, so we shut him into the other section for the night. Tony said this would give her time to adjust to her new surroundings.

Next morning, Tony went into the compound and looked through the window of the sleeping quarters and saw that Sheba was sniffing Snoopy through the partition's grille. He put them together, and as there was no fighting, left the ocelots alone. The trouble started when they were being fed. Snoopy stole all Sheba's food, even though he had plenty of his own. He has continued to do this ever since. Our solution to ensure that Sheba has enough food is to shut Snoopy up in a carrying case made of wire mesh in the enclosure and to feed them separately.

One day, it happened that for some reason Tony was

delayed in giving Sheba her food. Snoopy was already eating his in the wire box in the enclosure, so Sheba walked up to Snoopy, who was too engrossed in eating to notice her. His tail was sticking out from the wire mesh and Sheba bit it. As Snoopy sprung round to see what was happening, Sheba quickly put her paw into the wire box, snatched a piece of Snoopy's meat and ran with it in her mouth on to her shelf!

That winter was particularly cold and life by the river was especially bleak. Freezing north easterly winds blew straight off the water to buffet and chill us to the bone. The river looked grey and dismal, reflecting the winter sky and the only boats which we saw frequently were those belonging to the river police and the Thames Conservancy – those guardians of the river.

The cats' coats grew thicker than in summer and after a fall of snow, when the air was crisp, the sky blue and the sun shone, Snoopy would enjoy gambolling amidst it. Sometimes, Sheba would stretch and sit in the sunlit doorway of the sleeping hut watching him tossing the snow up in the air. Occasionally she would venture into the snow covered enclosure to sniff around for a few minutes before returning to the cosy warmth of her blankets beneath the heater. When the snow was falling, Snoopy would delight in chasing the snowflakes, trying to catch them in his mouth and looking surprised when they disappeared.

One night during that winter, the wind was gale force and blew so strongly that it lifted off part of the roof of the owls' aviary and sent it crashing to the ground, out of sight of the house. The rain was still pouring down as I left early the next morning and I did not notice that all was not well. A little later, Tony began his customary morning inspection of the animals and to his dismay, found three bedraggled owls forlornly standing on the grass in front of the aviary in the pelting rain. He quickly gathered them up and placed the birds in temporary accommodation. Then he looked for the missing owl, which was the youngster, and found him perched on a fence in our next-door neighbour's garden, with his feathers saturated with rain.

At Tony's approach, Baby Owl attempted to fly, but could not because his wings were waterlogged and consequently he flopped into the whirlpool in front of the weir. Tony watched with horror as the owl was sucked underneath the steel plates of the weir and into the maelstrom below. He ran to the other side of the weir and saw what appeared to be a dead bird being tossed and spun around in the seething water. Suddenly, he saw that its wings were weakly fluttering and as the bird was spun on to its back by the current, he could see its open eyes were moving and staring up at him. Then Baby Owl was caught in a back current, which swept him out of the maelstrom and around to the side of the weir into the island's backwater.

Instinctively, Tony dived into the river and had no difficulty in reaching the bird. Immediately his hand touched him, Baby Owl thrust his talons deep into Tony's flesh and clung on to him, but was not strong enough to sit upright and could only hang upside down with his wings brushing the water. The river was freezing Tony was so numb with cold that he did not feel any pain from the bird's sharp talons.

With only one arm free, he tried to swim towards the shore, but the current was pulling him so powerfully that he was in difficulties. Soon his arm began to ache with the strain of holding Baby Owl high above the water and he was rapidly feeling exhausted.

After what seemed to be a long time and with great effort, Tony finally managed to reach part of the weir's concrete walling, the top of which was about three feet above water level. He looked at Baby Owl, who was still hanging upside down, and saw, with relief, that he was still alive, with his wings weakly fluttering.

Tony began to shout for help, a neighbour heard but could not see him because he was beneath the wall and out of sight. Luckily, a resident on the mainland looked out of her bedroom window, saw him struggling in the water and came running over the bridge, still wearing bedroom slippers and dressing gown, to hold on to his jacket collar until stronger help arrived, and Tony and Baby Owl were pulled to safety.

Tony took the bird into the house and slowly and painfully managed to extract its talons from his hand and wrap it in a towel. The bird was very still with its eyes closed. Tony turned the electric oven on and when it was warm turned it off before placing the bird, still wrapped in the towel, on a wooden board, inside with the door open. As the blood was still streaming from his hand from the bird's sharp talons, he quickly bandaged it before filling a teaspoon with warm water, adding a few drops of brandy and glucose and giving it to Baby Owl which, together with the warmth of the oven, helped to revive him.

Gradually the young owl regained his strength and after three days intensive care, was strong enough to rejoin the rest of the colony and is still thriving today.

Snoopy relaxes in the undergrowth (*Copyright Colin Browne*)

Streaker puts his foot down (*Copyright Colin Browne*)

Fred and friend (*Copyright Colin Browne*)

Sheba (*Cop*

n Browne)

Poppet's hypnotic gaze (*Copyright Tony Travers*)

Marwell's magnificent tigers

Cleo inspects the final draft of my manuscript (*Copyright Tony Travers*)

Chapter Four

Like the ocelots, leopards are an endangered species and because of this and since the days of Prince, his leopard in Africa, Tony has always had a special affection and deep affinity for these animals.

He had found Prince after his mother had been shot for killing sheep. Prince's eyes were still closed and as he would not have survived without his mother, Tony took him home. As he disliked keeping a creature born in the jungle as a pet and a single animal away from its natural environment, he decided that when Prince was able to fend for himself to return him to the jungle. Prince grew rapidly into a powerful animal, one blow from which on the side of the head could have broken a human neck.

Tony made several journeys by car into the bush to look for a suitable place in which to release the leopard. On one such expedition, with a girlfriend, driving along the old, disused Gwanda Road in Rhodesia, they saw a little way ahead, a pride of lions blocking the road. Tony stopped the car and waited. The lions walked up to the car and surrounded it. One fully grown lion put his forelegs on to the window ledge and pressed a large, wet nose against the window and peered into the car. It looked docile enough and without thinking, Tony wound down the window about half an inch. Tony tickled the lion's nose as it sniffed at the gap in the window and the big cat sneezed which, Tony said, felt like being sprayed with a warm soda syphon. Suddenly, the lion hooked its claws onto the window glass and the winding handle spun round as the weight of the lion caused the window to open fully. Tony told his girlfriend to keep still but she had already fainted. Then the lion poked its head inside the car. Tony remained motionless as the lion sniffed him, licked his face, its tongue feeling like rough sandpaper, and then happily, lost interest and walked off to rejoin the rest of the pride which, by that time, were further along the road. Tony's body was covered with perspiration, he felt icy cold and remained sitting perfectly still unable to move for several minutes, thoroughly shaken.

Tony took Prince into the bush on several occasions to see how he would react. He would wander a little way from Tony, sniffing at the undergrowth, but kept looking round at him. When Tony stood still, Prince also stopped and then came loping back to sit beside him. Tony persevered, but while Prince was intrigued by the new sounds and smells around him, he would not let Tony out of his sight.

Tony was living in a crowded city and his flat soon became too small for the rapidly growing leopard. After much heart searching, Tony donated Prince to Johannesburg Zoo, a magnificent place where animals are kept in as near natural surroundings as possible and are very well treated. Here, Prince would have the companionship of his own kind. Tony decided not to go to see Prince because he felt that the meeting and especially the parting would be too upsetting for them both as they were very close.

Three years later, however, Tony had occasion to go to Johannesburg on business and against his better judgement went to see Prince. The leopard almost immediately recognised him, gave a deep throated rumble and walked straight over to rub himself against the bars nearest Tony, who immediately climbed over the protective rail. Tony put his arm into Prince's cage who began licking his hands and sucking his fingers, which was a habit acquired whilst he was being bottle fed by Tony as a cub. Tony stayed with Prince for the rest of the day, but when it was time to leave, Prince unsheathed his claws and gripped his arm, not to hurt him but to prevent him from leaving.

One day, Tony told me that the leopards from India were far smaller than the African ones. I should have known then that we were about to have yet another cat. He went on to tell me that he had heard of a female Indian leopard cub, aged eight weeks, which had been hand raised in Colchester Zoo, which is a splendid zoo and one of our favourites. The animals are beautifully kept in natural surroundings and the owners, Frank and Helena Farrar, have developed a unique relationship with them all.

The leopard cub was third generation born in this country, her parents were very tame and her father had appeared in several films. She was so sweet natured and gentle that her owners did not want her to end up in a concrete cage, but to go to someone who would take an interest in her.

Tony made arrangements to see the cub, which was called Poppy, and when he arrived at the zoo owners' house, she was upstairs with her companion, a black leopard cub of the same age but from another litter, which had also been hand raised. When called by Frank Farrar, two tiny faces peeped through the bannisters, one black, the other spotted. The two cubs then came running, tumbling and tripping down the long, wide staircase, playing 'touch' with each other. They landed with a bump on the hall floor, the black cub scampered away and Frank Farrar called Poppy who came over to him and to Tony. After greeting him, Poppy sniffed Tony for several moments and then rubbed herself against his leg. The feeling of affection was mutual and Tony bought her, but could not take her with him as she was too young.

A month later, Tony returned to collect Poppy by car, taking with him blankets and baby foods in a thermos flask as she still liked milk. She was put into a large travelling cage which was placed in the car in such a way that she could see Tony. During the homeward journey, she was restless and whimpered until Tony stopped the car and spoke softly to her for a long time to reassure her, stroking her through the wire of the travelling box and when she nuzzled his hand and relaxed, he continued the journey.

Three hours later, Tony and Poppy reached home and Tony called me to help him carry her box indoors. It was dark by then and all I could see were two luminous eyes gazing intently at me. I spoke softly to Poppy and her eyes never wavered from watching me unblinkingly. I felt nervous and wondered if I could really cope with a leopard but then, as I helped Tony with her box, my moment of apprehension passed. After such a long journey, Poppy was confused and therefore she would not, very understandably, come out of her box but remained at the end of it spitting.

As she did not know me, I thought that perhaps my presence might be worrying her so I left Tony alone with her. He fetched the choice pieces of meat which I had put out specially for her and gradually coaxed her out of her box. After a few minutes, Tony called me to come in, very slowly. I hesitated because I knew that even at this age, Poppy leopard cub could do damage with her teeth and claws. I took a deep breath and quietly and without haste, opened the door. I saw a cat with spots, huge feet, very chunky, about four times the size of Willy domestic cat, crouching on the floor. Her fur was dishevelled from the long journey as she had not cleaned herself. She spun round as I entered and spat but Tony told me to remain very still at first just inside the door and then slowly, very slowly, to sit down on the floor so that I was at Poppy's level because these cats do not like anyone towering over them. I sat down, well away from Poppy and started to talk softly and gently to her; very gradually she relaxed. I longed to stroke her but did not dare. I got up, again slowly, and fetched some milk, which I gave Tony to give her. She sniffed the milk, then drank it all and licked the empty dish so vigorously that I poured some more into another dish, but this time I gave it to her myself. As I put the dish down in front of her, Poppy looked up at me but did not spit. I edged away and sat down on the floor again and watched her. When she had finished drinking, she started to wash herself, and then to explore the kitchen, sniffing around. Tony told me that even more than with ocelots, one can only hope to be a comrade to leopards – they will not tolerate being bossed and I must respect her and not take liberties, especially when she was eating.

As Prince had slept with Tony, we had prepared a box for Poppy in our bedroom. Tony picked her up and carried her to the sleeping box, talking constantly to her. She inspected the box, sniffing and pushing the bedding around and then started to investigate the rest of the room. But she was tired after such a long day, and suddenly her legs would not move any more and she stretched, yawned and curled up on the floor. Tony picked her up and tenderly put her to bed in her box, she opened her eyes, looked up at us and then with a huge sigh, snuggled down and went to sleep. During the night, we were woken by whimpering and there was Poppy on the floor by our bed, looking up at Tony pathetically. After that, she spent the rest of the night in our bed, with her face wedged under Tony's armpit.

The next morning, I was woken by the sound of a river tug with a noisy engine, chugging by so rapidly that I could hear its wash smacking against our quay, and by the frenzied and obscene shouts of the coach as the young, strapping rowers, eight men to a long, thin and fragile looking boat, made mistakes. A little later, I looked out of the window and saw a faint haze over the river and the newly risen sun shining through it on to the shimmering water and then I looked at Tony and there was Poppy, still sound asleep, with one paw over his neck. She awoke, yawned, stretched, spreading her huge paws to show her claws and began to fidget so much that she woke Tony. He watched her for a few moments and then got out of bed, picked her up and carried her to the large toilet tray, which I had taken the precaution of putting on newspaper to absorb any miscalculations. I had put some of Willy's urine into it to show what the tray was meant for. Poppy sniffed it once and used the tray properly – which she has continued to do ever since.

By this time, Tony was in the bathroom shaving. Poppy followed hesitantly and gradually inched one eye and flattened ear round the bathroom door, and immediately backed quickly at the sight of Tony whom she did not recognise with lather round his chin. Tony saw her disappear and quickly finished shaving and found her outside the bathroom door, looking forlorn. He picked her up and carried her into the lounge and made her comfortable on the settee. Tony told me that he did not want Poppy to go out for a couple of days at least, but to remain in the house quietly to adjust to her new home and to recover from the long car journey. During that day, she followed him around the house whenever she could and paid little attention to me. I have found that as I do not have the same deep affinity for most animals as Tony has, my best and easiest way of gaining their confidence is to give them food and drink, which I did with Poppy. During the following days, I saw there was a very close bond forming between them and without consciously being aware of doing so, Tony started to call her Poppet as a term of endearment, and the name stuck.

Physically, Poppet was very different to Snoopy. Poppet's bones were thicker, heavier and stronger than Snoopy's whose bone structure, by comparison, was fine and slender. Poppet's head was wide at the top and did not taper to such a fine point at the chin as did Snoopy's narrower face. Her nose was broad and her eyes were in proportion to her face whereas Snoopy's eyes were big. Poppet's tail was thick and almost the same length as her body, but Snoopy's tail was much shorter and thinner. I was to learn later that a margay, which closely resembles an ocelot, has a tail which touches the ground with a slight curl at the end, whilst an ocelot's tail does not reach the floor and is straight. The margay is much smaller than the ocelot, but its eyes in proportion to its head, are huge.

On the third day after her arrival, Poppet was so lively that Tony decided to take her outside into the summer sun. It took some time to secure the collar round her neck as she wanted to play with it and I had to distract her while Tony fastened it. He attached the lead and coaxed her to the front door. She jibbed at the top of the three steps leading down into the garden; the steps are high because the house is built on stilts as the River Thames is at the bottom of the garden a few yards away. Poppet sat down, her eyes grew larger and rounder as she looked around. The distance between the steps was too great for her and Tony lifted her down and put her on the lawn. She immediately started sniffing the grass and found a drowsy bee. She prodded it with her paw and jumped back as it moved, but then our neighbours' tiny dachshund, Jester, came bounding through a hole in the fence and the bee which I had quickly removed to a place of safety, was forgotten.

Jester's tail was quivering with curiosity at Poppet, he barked defensively, turned and ran towards the rockery,

Poppet leapt after him, pulling at the lead. Tony allowed her to follow the dog at a distance and then I distracted her, on Tony's instructions, by moving my hand amongst some tall grass, making them rustle. Tony let the lead out to its full length and Poppet crouched, her head down, her ears flattened, preparing to spring and then leapt in one long, flowing movement towards my hand. Just before she landed, I felt a flash of apprehension – supposing she broke my hand or tore it? I took it away quickly. Tony shouted at me that I should never pull away from one of these cats, but let my hand go to and with them; it is pulling away that one gets scratched.

When Jester had gone, we quickly repaired the hole in the fence and let Poppet off the lead. Tony and I sat on the grass and pretended not to see her as she stalked us from behind the rockery, crouching down so that just the top of her head was showing, her ears flattened. She then rushed us, bumping Tony with her head. When she was older, my head was once accidentally in collision with hers and it felt as if I was being hit by a thick concrete slab.

I brought morning coffee into the garden and included on the tray a bowl of milk, with one egg and vitamins for Poppet and gave it to her myself. She was excited by this time and gulped the milk. As Tony did not want her to become too tired, we took her back indoors. She spent the rest of the morning playing with a toilet roll, which she shredded over the lounge before falling asleep on the settee.

I had let Snoopy out into the enclosure earlier that morning and as he was by himself at the time, I gave him either raw carrots or hard-boiled eggs to play with to prevent him becoming bored. He was always instantly aware of the slightest movement in the garden and had been watching Poppet from the moment she appeared on the steps. He had sprung up on to the high shelf in the enclosure from which he could see her clearly. He stood absolutely still, with only his eyes moving as he followed her movements. Suddenly Poppet saw him too. Immediately she froze, crouched on her stomach and after a few moments began to run forward for a few steps to the honeysuckle bush immediately in front of the enclosure. We could see that even though she had been hand raised, the instinct to stalk was very strong. Snoopy lost sight of her behind the bush and jumped down from the high shelf and sped to the end of the run to spring, in one effortless, liquid movement, on to the shelf again to try to see her, but he could not, and began to climb the wire.

At that moment, one eye, half a spotted face with its broad, flat nose and pure white, strong whiskers looked round the bush. Poppet gazed at Snoopy for a few seconds and then the rest of her appeared as she cautiously moved towards the enclosure. The two animals tentatively sniffed each other through the wire and gradually Snoopy's whiskers moved back to their relaxed position flat against his face and Poppet's whiskers relaxed too. Then, disgracefully, Snoopy turned his back and sprayed urine. His aim was accurate and it caught poor Poppet full in the face. She jumped back and Tony picked her up whilst I wiped her face. Since then, Snoopy has ceased to exist for her and if she does happen to walk by his enclosure, she gives no sign of acknowledging his presence, though he tries to attract her attention by rushing round and jumping up at the wire.

I did not allow Snoopy into the kitchen because he was very fast and tended to spring suddenly, from a standing position, several feet off the ground, onto shelves scattering their contents. Poppet was much slower and heavier than Snoopy and did not jump up as he did and therefore we allowed her, whilst we were in the house, to wander through several rooms, including the kitchen but not when I was cooking. A few days later, I noticed that my potatoes were rapidly disappearing mysteriously. Then I caught Poppet playing football with one. From then on, I kept a supply aside for her in a special bowl which she could easily reach.

Gradually, I gained Poppet's confidence and this was initiated by giving her food. At least once a day, I fed her by hand so that she became used to my scent and during this period I did not wear perfume as I thought this might confuse her. I sat with her often, talking to her, but somehow I instinctively felt it would be wrong to muss her or to have the same rough and tumble I had had with Snoopy.

I have found that I get on better with male animals than with females. I can relax with them and they with me in a way which I never can with female animals, with the exception of female Willy, the domestic cat, but then she is neutred. People have sometimes asked me whether animals can tell the difference between male and female humans and I have no doubt that the cats can. If a female cat forms an attachment to Tony, I am always wary and treat her with respect because I know that in her eyes, I am the opposing female and that she might harm me, given the opportunity. I have tried to counteract this by always being the one to feed the females, but I am still ultra-cautious – female jealousy over a male is very strong, whether animal or human. In later years, when Poppet became adult, she would be extremely jealous of me as the usurping female with Tony's affections, but for the moment she was a little cub which I could pick up occasionally.

It soon became an established routine at night for Poppet to use her toilet tray, jump on to our bed, romp round for a few minutes and then, with a gigantic sigh, flop down between us fast asleep. Normally, I am the first to rise in the mornings and when Poppet realised this, she would place her paw on to my face at about half past six and nuzzle me until I got out of bed. She never touched Tony at this time.

One problem which I had with Poppet was that she would insist on jumping up at me when I was carrying full dishes and cups. This happened several times as I was carrying the breakfast porridge from the kitchen, resulting in smashed crockery and porridge over the floor. I soon learnt that just as Poppet was springing towards me, to show her that I was carrying full dishes of porridge and to say firmly, "Don't jump up!" Poppet, in turn, soon began when she saw the porridge, to skid to a halt and then jump away without touching the dishes. I like to think that she was trying to save me mopping up yet more mess, but perhaps it really was that she just did not like my cooking!

One day, Poppet jumped on top of a glass-fronted cabinet full of my mother's valuable antique china. Her weight was too much for it and Tony and I watched with horror as the cabinet tottered and then fell slowly forward wedging halfway against a settee, breaking one of the glass panels. Tony dashed forward to prevent the cabinet from falling any further. The china was in a jumbled heap inside and I took it out as he supported the cabinet but as I was doing this, the valuable china cascaded to the ground and smashed. Poppet had, by this time, wisely disappeared under the settee. Amongst the smashed china was my mother's best tea service, tea cups with broken handles, treasured pieces from her girlhood days, lay in fragments. It was then that we realised the value of having a tube of glue in the house and we sat on the floor until three o'clock in the morning trying to stick handles back on those cups which remained unbroken.

Poppet's attachment to Tony grew as she became older, and his to her, but I thought that she and I were good friends. However, one night, when I was in bed, Poppet sat on my head and urinated over me. My hair was dripping, the urine running down my face, much to Tony's amusement.

Fortunately, the urine of these jungle cats is not offensive and smells pleasantly woody, unlike that of the domestic cat. I am still not sure whether her action was that of like or dislike. She has never urinated on Tony's head though she has had ample opportunity.

As with Snoopy, we took Poppet, while she was a cub, out in the car occasionally and once I had to meet Tony at the television studios where Fred Owl was being filmed. Members of the cast had said that they would like to see young Poppet, so I took her along in my car. She behaved very well, the cast gathered round and petted her but she was not filmed.

On the way home, I was driving behind Tony and saw in front of us that the sky was heavy with dark rain clouds. Then we drove into the storm, the hailstones beat down on to the roof of my car, the lightning flashed, the thunder rumbled then cracked loudly overhead and I thought that it was enough to make any animal, however tame, go beserk. As there was no other traffic on the road, I slowed the car and quickly looked round at Poppet who was sitting on the back seat, her eyes wide with fear. I thought that if Poppet were to go into Tony's car, it might be dangerous transferring her from one car to another if there is lightning and thunder just as we are doing it. She might, through fear, rip the upholstery of Tony's expensive car and anyway Fred Owl was loose sitting on the back of Tony's seat and it would take time to transfer him into his carrying box. It would be far better for Poppet to remain in my old car and for Tony to drive it so that he could reassure her. I looked for him to flash with my lights to suggest this, but he had disappeared round a bend in the road and I was alone with a frightened leopard who was capable of killing me if she jumped up from behind as I was driving and tore at my throat. I stopped the car and told myself to keep calm. I slowly turned round and faced Poppet, hoping that she would not jump at my face. She looked at me pathetically and made a peculiar sound in the back of her throat, like someone with laryngitis trying to speak, which I had not heard her make before. I spoke softly to her, saying her name and telling her to stay perfectly still, then the lightning flashed and the thunder cracked immediately overhead and Poppet flinched. I stroked her and as the lightning flashed again, I pressed my hand lightly into her back and told her it was all right in what I hoped was a reassuring tone because by this time I was becoming frightened myself. Suddenly, I heard a car hoot, and there was Tony. Poppet saw him, whimpered once and lifted her front paws on to the back of my seat so that she could have a better view of him. He came running to the car, rain streaming down his face, opened my door and put his hand inside to fondle Poppet, who rubbed herself against him. I suggested changing cars to which Tony agreed. I slid over to the passenger seat and Tony got in. Poppet immediately put her front paws over his shoulders and started licking his face and hair. I quietly got out of the car, whereupon Poppet jumped into my vacated seat and climbed on to Tony's lap. I sprinted to Tony's car, Fred Owl whistled at me as I got in and I stroked his chest feathers and gently blew into them for several minutes until Tony hooted at me that he was ready to drive off home.

Later that evening, Poppet was more affectionate towards me than usual and licked my hand for some time, her tongue feeling like rough sandpaper.

At the bottom of our garden, moored on the River Thames, we had a fifty-foot boat, which had been designed by the first owner some twenty years previously. Its bow was flared, its lines were good, but it had been neglected. The for'ard section was divided into two large cabins with the bridge, engine room and toilet in the middle of the boat, then a companionway leading to the bathroom and another toilet and finally the gallery and rear cabin. Above the main bridge there was a flying bridge with a wide, flat roof. Sometimes we took Poppet on board with us while we were renovating and put her in the front section so that she could run around without coming to any harm and be near us, or rather Tony, at the same time. Often Tony would put her on a lead and take her on deck in the sun.

Following her leopard's natural instinct to be as high as possible, Poppet's favourite place was on the flat roof of the flying bridge, where she could watch the boats going by. It was amusing to watch the expressions on the faces of the boats' occupants when they saw Poppet, and more especially if they did not notice her until they were level with our boat and were startled to suddenly look up to see a leopard eyeing them.

On one occasion, a luxurious steel boat sailed past, the owner looking in disbelief at Poppet. He turned his boat around and came alongside to have another look at the leopard watching him. Tony said with a straight face, "We have to keep a large cat as there are big rats round here!"

Sheba also went onto the boat while we were working there. This was a satisfactory arrangement because Sheba took it in turns with Poppet to be on the boat with us or, very occasionally, Poppet would be shut in the front section with Sheba in the rear cabin, while Tony and I worked in the middle on the bridge.

As our boat had not been used by the previous owners for about a year, there was much dirt and dust and many spiders aboard. When I complained of the spiders, Tony said that at least they were not poisonous, and told me of an incident that occurred while he was staying in Southern Rhodesia.

He was living in a rondawel, which is a round, mud hut with a thatched roof, and after a few days he noticed that a large spider had woven its web in the eaves. The spider was the size of a man's thumbnail and had four spots on its back, like a button. When a light shone on the spider at certain angles, its eyes were pink and glowing.

Tony cut meat into fine slivers and placed these in the spider's web each day. At first it waited until Tony had moved to the far end of the hut before taking the meat. After a few days, it started, at first cautiously, to venture towards him while he was placing the food in its web until finally, the spider took the meat from Tony's fingers. It then extended its web and wove the anchor line on to Tony's bed rail. At feeding time, it ran down the anchor line to take the meat from his fingers. During the following weeks, the spider became bolder, running along the bed rail to take its food from Tony and sometimes running over the back of his hand before scuttling back to its web.

One day, a South African friend called to see Tony and while they were quietly relaxing over a drink, the friend suddenly, without warning, grabbed a slipper and frantically beat the spider to death before Tony could stop him.

It was only then that he learnt that he had been living with and feeding a poisonous button spider. However, he is convinced that provided he had not molested the spider, it would not have harmed him.

By this time, Snoopy was living outside in the garden with Sheba, as the isolation, in quiet peaceful surroundings, would enable them to become acquainted with one another and to mate. However, although they settled down well together, and mated, Sheba did not conceive. This may have been because Snoopy was still too young to be a father.

As Tony and I wanted to get to know Sheba, we had her in the house for varying periods while Poppet was in her outdoor daytime run to take advantage of the summer sun. Sheba settled down so well that we assumed she had lived in a house before.

It so happened that a regular visitor had a beard, and

whenever Sheba saw him, she went straight up to him, climbed onto his lap and started nuzzling his beard, gently pulling and licking it. Somewhere in her past, there must have been a bearded man of whom she was very fond. Our bearded friend, Commander Mike Roberts, responded to her, rubbing her under the chin, scratching her head and talking softly to her.

Another visitor did not have the same rapport with Sheba as Commander Roberts had. He arrived whilst we were working on the boat, and Tony told him that Sheba was on board, in the saloon, but as she was asleep the visitor ventured on board and sat on the settee. However Sheba woke up and decided to investigate the stranger. He did not notice her move at first until she was by his feet looking up at him. He stopped talking and stiffened. Sheba jumped on to the settee, which was one of her favourite sleeping spots. Tony told him not to move and to relax as Sheba would not harm him. But when he leaned forward to take a cigarette from Tony, Sheba put her front paws onto his sloping back and sniffed the back of his neck. His face went ashen, his hands trembled, so I coaxed her away with a piece of meat and shut her in the bathroom. As he was leaving the boat, Poppet Leopard, who happened to be on board as it was a cold, sunless day, rattled the handle of the locked door leading to her front cabin. I told our visitor that it was a leopard, but he laughed and did not seem to believe me, so when we were on the quay, I called Poppet, who poked her head out of the porthole and looked at him. We did not see him again!

One day, Sheba was missing on the boat. I was painting and she had been sleeping on the settee in the saloon for most of the afternoon but when I went to look for her, she was not there. I searched all her favourite places, but could not find her. Suddenly, I heard a scratching noise coming from the engine room. I opened the hatch and out crawled a black Sheba, most of her fur was covered in oil and grease and she smelt of diesel. The rest of the afternoon was spent in cleaning her with detergent, soap and water.

Tony eventually received a letter from the pet shop in New York which had sold Sheba to us, saying that her name in America had been Pepper. We tried calling her that with both American and English accents, but with no response. So we continued to call her Sheba.

She is still noisy and I know, without looking, when she is eating and drinking because of the gurgling and 'yummy' sounds. She is very clean and obviously used to a toilet tray, but will insist afterwards on squatting, then shuffling forward on her bottom, wiping it on the floor or on the carpet!

Tony discovered that if he unbuttoned the front of his jacket, when sitting down, Sheba would crawl inside and try to worm her way round to his back. She is too big for this now and has to shuffle backwards, emerging to sit on his lap. One wonders who taught her to do this.

5—SFS • •

Chapter Five

When Poppet Leopard was just under a year old, Tony and I had to go away and Poppet stayed with a man with a great love for animals. Snoopy, Sheba and the owls were looked after by friends with vast experience of these animals, who lived near us, but sadly, within about a year, they were to move away.

While Poppet was away, there was an accident and she was bitten in the right foot by another leopard and two toes had to be amputated. Unfortunately, the vet. who attended her lacked the experience so essential in treating these cats and did not sedate her sufficiently and she began to gnaw her leg, which eventually became gangrenous and had to be amputated at the shoulder.

Tony would wake up in the middle of the night with what we think must have been a telepathic pain in his elbow. This became so bad that regularly, night after night, I had to give him a pain-killing tablet. Tony has a horror of hospitals and doctors after some bad experiences during the war and is, therefore, very reluctant to seek their help. Eventually the pain was so bad that he was forced to make an appointment at a hospital on the morning of which he was advised by the vet. that Poppet would have to be destroyed, since all the unnecessary pain she had suffered would probably make her revert and become wild and vicious.

When we went to see her, we found that Poppet had, in her pain, bitten off about half her tail and was still chewing at the remaining stump. Tony went inside the leopard's quarters and saw Poppet lying on a ledge just staring into space. He called her name, once, and directly she heard his voice she looked across at him, cried out and very slowly got up on her three legs, wobbled, regained her balance and reached the floor, then she hobbled over to Tony whimpering. Tony asked to be let inside the cage, then knelt down, drew Poppet on to his lap and put his arms round her. Poppet constantly whimpered and licked Tony. Tony called me and I could see that he was visibly distressed and almost in tears. I had expected to see Poppet in a far worse condition. I went inside the cage but was advised by the keepers not to go too near her as they thought she might turn on me. She looked at me and whimpered and I knelt down beside Tony and put my arms round Poppet and kissed the top of her head. She licked me and then returned to nuzzling Tony. We looked at the remains of her tail, the end of which was raw bone. Tony suggested that we took her home in the car. Gently and very tenderly, he lifted Poppet off his lap and placed her on the ground. When we left to fetch the car, Poppet must have thought that we were abandoning her because when we reached the outside of the building and were out of her sight, she started to 'scream' without stopping. I went back to comfort her and wait with her until Tony arrived with the car. The keeper said that he had never heard an animal cry like that and we will never forget her anguish when she thought we were leaving without her.

The keeper opened the cage door and Poppet hobbled out, resting every few yards until Tony lifted her up and carried her to the car. I did not sit by her in case the car lurched or stopped suddenly and I bumped against her shoulder or raw tail. She constantly chewed at the protruding tail bones and later, when we cleaned the car, we found blood and several pieces of her bone there. Tony carried her over the bridge to the island, and then to our garden gate. She was heavy and as Tony has an old spinal injury which is aggravated if he carries heavy weights, he was forced to put her down in the garden. We expected her to make for the house but instead she hobbled towards the boat. We helped her on board and she immediately made her way to the large front cabins which she knew. After we had made her as comfortable as we could, we left the boat to collect the blankets, food and milk waiting for her in the house. As I walked down the gangplank behind Tony, Poppet put her head out of the porthole, looked at us and whimpered continuously. I returned to her and sat comforting her while Tony went into the house.

Tony telephoned our animals' vet. and after a long discussion with him and also with the R.S.P.C.A.'s chief vet. it was decided that as Poppet had such a wonderful nature, everything possible should be done to try to save her. After all, a human being is not destroyed if he loses a limb. Our vet. immediately prescribed antibiotic injections prior to cutting back her tail and re-flapping it, which Tony had to administer. It was arranged that this operation should take place three days later on the boat as the atmosphere of a vet.'s surgery would have been too traumatic after Poppet's recent horrific ordeal of amputation in a similar place. We slept on board the boat that night, but not with Poppet in case we rolled over on to her wounds whilst asleep, but we left all the doors open so that she could come into us if she wished. And she did, spending the night lying on the floor by Tony's bunk.

I was out at work when the operation was performed and Tony told me about it afterwards. He had cleaned out the saloon and disinfected it as the vet. instructed and had a suitable table ready and plenty of hot water, and started off sedating Poppet. The vet. arrived to find Poppet in a drowsy state, but nowhere near unconscious, so he had to give her another injection, after which he sat on the settee. Poppet was lying about four yards away in the companion-way. As the anaesthetic started to take effect, the vet. turned to look at her and Poppet, with one tremendous leap, sprang at him. As she did, the vet. leant forward and she fell down at the back of him on to the settee in deep tranquillity. They then lifted her on to the table and local anaesthetic was injected all round the tail to block the nerves. When it was finished and the tip of her tail was bandaged, they carried her back to the front cabin and made her comfortable. The vet. decided to keep her under sedation as long as it was safe to do so. Every twelve hours, Tony would cut back on the injection sufficiently to bring her round to enough consciousness to hold her by the scruff of her neck, support her and 'lump' her up and down for about a quarter of an hour to keep her circulation going and to prevent any chance of pneumonia setting in. Then he placed her back on her bed and sedated her again. This treatment was continued for ten days, after which it was necessary to withdraw any further sedation because of the risk of pneumonia and heart failure.

As soon as Poppet was no longer under sedation, she pulled off the white bandage and chewed her tail removing the flap which our vet. had so carefully stitched. I was by myself, Tony was out, and I wondered if she was starting to eat herself again. I tried to pull her head away from her tail, but she turned and snarled at me. So I sat on the floor, about three feet away, and every time Poppet chewed her tail, I shouted, "No!" and gently tapped her nose with a newspaper. She did not take any notice of me at first, but I was persistent and talked softly and soothingly to her between the shouts, and gradually, she stopped chewing so hard and so often. Then Tony returned, examined the stump and got a bottle of Cicatrin powder from his animals' medicine cupboard. This has an amino acid base, which is very beneficial in forming tissue. While I distracted Poppet, Tony sprinkled the Cicatrin powder on to her raw stump. Poppet sprung round and started licking the tail. We both shouted at her and told her to leave it alone. At the sound of Tony's voice, Poppet looked round at him and then stretched out on the floor. Tony sprinkled some more Cicatrin on to her tail, which she licked, but not very hard so that some of the powder remained. He continued this treatment, with our vet.'s approval, for many weeks until the tail started, very slowly, to heal.

In the weeks that followed, Poppet gradually became used to balancing on only three legs. The vet. and Tony felt that the boat was a good place for her because it restricted her movements to a certain extent thus avoiding the remaining front leg becoming overstrained. In time, it became stronger and able to cope with the weight of her body. Poppet recovered so well that Tony took her into the garden on sunny days to romp on the lawn. Someone, however, did not agree with us and reported Poppet's condition to the R.S.P.C.A. We have been grateful to them ever since because, through this, we met W. J. (Bill) Jordan, Deputy Chief Veterinary Officer with the society. The informer first approached our local R.S.P.C.A. inspector who did not have any experience with leopards and therefore passed the complaint on to his headquarters. Tony invited Bill Jordan to see Poppet.

At their meeting, she sniffed him and then vigorously licked his new, spotless, pale fawn-coloured suede shoes, leaving stains. Tony offered to buy him a new pair, but Bill laughingly refused. A few days later, we received the following letter from Bill Jordan, " . . . Your animals and birds are in good condition and well cared for. It is obvious from the way these wild animals allow you to handle them that there is a mutual affection present. I was sorry to hear the history of the injuries your leopard suffered. However, she has a great affection for you and her romps in the garden afford sufficient exercise. The ocelots show no signs of boredom, or lack of exercise, so obviously they do not spend all their time in the pen. They are well fed and in good condition. I hope you are successful in getting them to breed."

Shortly after, Professor Leyhausen of the Max-Planck Institut, Germany, one of the leading authorities in the world on the wild species of cats, visited us and said that in all his experience he had never seen such rapport between a human and a leopard as there was between Tony and Poppet.

Tony felt that Poppet would not become bored whilst on the boat because she could look out of the portholes on to the river on the one side and at the garden and house on the other. I was interested to notice that one particular swan used to paddle up to the boat and stretch its beak up to within a few inches of Poppet's head looking out of the porthole. This happened many times and I never saw the swan hiss at her nor she spit at the swan.

I tried to make friends with this swan as I remembered Tony telling me that before we had met he had had a tame swan. When his boat was moored on the Thames at Kingston he used to feed the ducks and swans which eventually became so tame that they tapped on the hull of his boat for food as early as half past six in the morning.

One day Tony noticed that a particular swan had a bottom beak which extended about an inch beyond the top. This deformity prevented it from feeding properly and Tony decided to take it to a veterinary surgeon for treatment. As the boat was moored on piles some way from the shore, he had to use a rowing boat and after a struggle, he managed to haul the sick swan aboard. He rowed the swan ashore, and on dry land lifted the bird from the boat with both arms round its body. As he was by himself, there was nobody to control the swan's long neck, which weaved backwards and forwards like a cobra.

The swan honked at everyone they met. As he walked along a narrow alley towards the vet.'s surgery, Tony met a woman wearing a straw hat, on the brim of which were masses of artificial cherries. When they drew level, the swan suddenly lunged forward and tried to snatch the gleaming red cherries. The woman shrieked and fled, tightly clutching her hat.

The vet. told Tony to come back for the swan in the afternoon. When Tony returned, a very drowsy swan was waiting, its beak having been cut back. Tony began to carry the swan back towards the river, but they had not progressed very far when the swan struggled to be put down. Immediately its feet touched the ground, the bird waddled away, swaying slightly from side to side from the effects of the anaesthetic, into the street market with Tony in hot pursuit trying to catch it amongst the stalls and shoppers' legs. Eventually Tony caught the swan and gathered it up into his arms once more, the shoppers and stall keepers staring and nudging each other in amusement.

They set off again towards the river but when the swan smelt the water, it again struggled from Tony's arms onto the ground and made off as fast as it could. Just before it flopped into the water, it turned its head and glared at Tony. The swan was not seen for five days, though Tony searched, but on the sixth day, it was back among the rest of the birds round the boat in the early morning.

From that day, the swan followed Tony whenever it could. This became embarrassing as it accompanied him to the pub and when his car was being repaired, the swan escorted him to the bus stop and waited until he boarded the bus before returning to the river and it was always waiting for Tony to return in the rowing boat with his food shopping and followed him back to the big boat.

One day, Tony happened to leave some loose biscuits in a bag on top of his shopping. The swan stretched its long neck into the boat, investigated the shopping, found the biscuits and ate them. As it obviously enjoyed them and searched for more, Tony always, from then on, bought an extra bag of broken biscuits especially for the swan.

Tony's swan was a pen and when she eventually mated she built a nest on a disused slipway. She laid a clutch of eggs and when she was sitting on her nest, Tony was able to sit quietly by her, stroking her and talking to her with the cob standing only a few feet away watching. After she had been on the nest for about a week, Tony returned to find that in his absence, her eggs had been stolen and the nest set alight. The cob had vanished, but the poor pen was still there by the smouldering remains of her nest with her feathers singed and her feet blistered. She would not let Tony near her and when he tried to catch her to try to help because she was so badly burnt, she went down the slipway into the water and paddled away, never to return.

When Tony took the boat out for a trip on the river, Poppet, of course, came as well causing quite a stir amongst the other boat owners, especially at the locks. She became friendly with the various lock-keepers, who always talked to her, but she disliked the boat being taken through the locks. She would look out of her porthole and spit at the 'moving' lock wall as the water rose or fell; then when the boat was stationary waiting for the lock to fill or empty and Tony and I were on the lock wall handling the ropes, she would pop her head out of a porthole and call out to Tony, looking at him intently and anxiously.

Her call can best be translated into human speech as sounding like the word 'owl' in a surprisingly low tone for such a large cat. At these times, if Tony or I were at the bow or stern of the boat and not very near her, the lock-keepers would talk to her to reassure her that all was well.

One day, the boat was moored just outside a lock and I heard the lock-keeper call to some people in a rowing boat not to go too near our boat as there was a leopard on board. I was down below and could not see them, but I knew that they had disregarded the advice because, suddenly, there was a scream from the woman as Poppet poked her head out of a porthole, apparently just above their heads.

On sunny days, Poppet liked to go out onto the aft deck to lie in the sun and as she became stronger she would leap, once again, on to her favourite place on the roof of the flying bridge to watch the boats, but when she saw boys in kyack canoes, she would rush below. Tony had to comfort her and she would not go on deck again until long after the canoes had disappeared. We can only think that these boys had gone too close to her portholes with their paddles and frightened her.

Poppet was also frightened of people dressed entirely in white. It so happened that a neighbour was working on his car and came into the garden, dressed in white overalls to borrow some tools from Tony. Poppet was on deck with Tony and directly she saw the white clothed figure coming towards them, she ran below as fast as she could, trembling, and rushed into a corner. Tony spent at least half an hour calming her. We realised that the last time she had seen a white clothed figure advancing towards her had been at the vet.'s surgery when her leg had been amputated. Poppet also dislikes people near her wearing red, which we think she associates with blood, again from the amputation operation and the subsequent severing of her tail. Occasionally her claws, especially her dew claw, would catch one of us when we were playing with her and we bled, but Poppet never minded our blood and usually licked Tony's scratches and sometimes mine.

Once a week I put disinfectant in the animals' toilet trays and Willy's tray somehow became mixed up with Poppet's on the boat. When I realised this, I put Willy's tray on the deck in readiness to be taken ashore. Poppet had been romping in the garden and on returning to the boat, saw Willy's tray. She sniffed it, realised what it was for and automatically used it. It was amusing to see a huge leopard trying to use a domestic cat's small toilet tray.

When Poppet was just over two years old, she went into season for the first time. I have been told since that a leopard in season is highly dangerous but I did not know this at the time. I was alone in the boat when I heard a noise, like someone sawing wood, coming from Poppet's cabin. I investigated and found her rolling around on the floor making this 'sawing' noise. She wound herself round my feet and was very friendly. However, Tony and the vet. felt it best that I did not go in to her again by myself when she was in season.

One day, Tony and I planned to drive down to Southampton to see a boat, but before we had travelled very far, Tony stopped the car and said that he felt that there was something wrong at home. I agreed that we should return having had experience of Tony's correct hunches before. When we arrived home, we found Poppet lying on the cabin floor whimpering. She had damaged her back legs whilst romping around – or perhaps some boys in canoes had paddled right up to the boat and frightened her so that she jumped away from the portholes clumsily. Tony examined her and found, thankfully, that she had not broken any bones, but had twisted and wrenched some muscles. She looked so pathetic pulling herself along the floor on her remaining front leg.

I fetched some blankets and Tony made a bed for her on the floor and began to massage her back legs. I telephoned the vet. who came the same day and after examining Poppet confirmed that no bones were broken, gave Tony some tablets to keep her under light sedation and told him to continue with the massage. After many hours of Tony's massaging, Poppet's hind legs slowly became less painful until she was able to walk on them again.

When Poppet was fully recovered and was able to leap and land without difficulty, Tony built an enclosure and sleeping hut for her in the garden facing the river so that she could still watch the boats as well as the house. We felt it essential that as she was a single animal, with a disablement, she should not become bored.

The affinity between Tony and Poppet grew and to this day remains wonderfully strong. She makes her soft 'owl' sound when she sees him, which he answers with a similar sound and this 'conversation' will continue for several minutes; Poppet never 'speaks' to me in this way. Sometimes, when Tony goes in to her, she pulls him to her and sucks his shirt vigorously, licks his hair and is especially fond of biting holes in his socks.

Our neighbour, Eddie Messer, also has a very close association with Poppet. He talks affectionately to her and she responds by rolling over and over on her back to show him her stomach, with a soft expression in her eyes, which changes to a dark, hard look if I go near.

On a couple of occasions, Poppet has knocked away the upright metal bar supporting the ledge in her outside run, and it was necessary to re-weld this. When Tony built her sleeping hut, he cut a small opening in the door so that Poppet could easily go in and out at will, but the disadvantage is that we cannot shut her in. Consequently, she was outside when Tony took a portable welding outfit in to her enclosure to re-weld the bar. Directly Tony started welding, Poppet ran into her den away from the sparks, and although she was, naturally, nervous she was not terrified because of her trust in Tony.

One of Poppet's favourite tricks when Tony goes in to clean her enclosure is to knock him down, then sit on his chest licking his face, or when he is bending over, to jump onto his back. Tony is able to stroke her when she is eating, when leopards are normally most dangerous. Unhappily, as Poppet has grown older, she has become jealous of me, regarding me as a usurping female with Tony's affections. She snarls at me whenever she thinks Tony is not in sight, but if Tony is with me, she licks me as if she likes me. If I do go into her enclosure with Tony, never by myself now, she will tolerate me there for about two minutes, then her eyes blacken as she looks at me and if I do not go immediately, she chases me out giving me a nip with her small front teeth.

During this time Snoopy and Sheba were mating regularly, with Sheba continually aborting, usually at the fifth week. During mating, the back of the female ocelot's neck is badly ripped by the male's claws and teeth. After one such vicious mating, the wounds on Sheba's neck began to turn septic. It happened that Tony was talking on the telephone that morning to Reg and Pam Matta, our friends from Sheba's quarantine days, and told them about Sheba's septic neck. Reg and Pam were preparing to go for a day's picnic in the country with their children, but on hearing of Sheba's condition, said that they would come down to us bringing with them Terramycin antibiotic in the form of an aerosol spray. Sheba disliked the hiss of the spray but after much coaxing, allowed Tony to spray her neck with purple coloured anti-biotic, which healed the wounds successfully.

Using the knowledge he had gleaned after ten years with animals in Africa, Tony put Sheba, with our vet.'s approval, on a course of special treatment and diet directly after the mating. Some forty days later, we noticed that she was putting on weight. Tony separated the ocelots so as to give Sheba extra nourishment, vitamins and peace away from

Snoopy. The normal gestation period for ocelots is ninety days and by the eighty-ninth day, Sheba was so fat and sluggish that we knew that birth was imminent. Tony contacted the vet. and it was decided to leave Sheba to give birth alone; if disturbed, she might eat the kit.

The next morning I awoke early and without waking Tony, quietly went into the garden to Sheba's sleeping quarters. As my eyes became accustomed to the half light, I saw a few spots of blood on the blankets. Sheba was lying down. I spoke softly to her, she raised her head with a soft expression in her eyes and then looked down. I followed her gaze and there, between her paws, saw a tiny ball of fur.

I rushed back to the house and fetched Tony, who went inside the compound and slowly approached Sheba. I stayed outside looking through the window. Sheba allowed Tony to touch her kit with his little finger. Tony told me afterwards that he was a little afraid to feel the kit in case it was dead. As he gently stroked it, the kit moved and Sheba started to lick it – the first ocelot to be born alive in England. Tony gave Sheba some milk and meat and as she had already cleaned the kit, left her to sleep. He telephoned the vet. who, after hearing his report, said that as all seemed well, he would not see Sheba for a couple of days as his presence might disturb her as she did not know him very well. I did not venture inside Sheba's sleeping quarters either thinking she might not like another female to be so near. That evening, Tony gave Sheba some more food and milk, saw that the kit was suckling satisfactorily, and left them alone, after making her comfortable for the night.

The following day, Tony saw, with horror, that Sheba was walking around the enclosure carrying the kit with its head entirely in her mouth and the body dangling. Tony thought she was eating it. He raced inside the enclosure, Sheba ceased walking around, sat at his feet and looked up at him with such a gentle expression in her eyes that he sat down on the ground with her. Immediately, Sheba placed her kit on his lap. She then stretched herself across his legs and watched them both through sleepy half-closed eyes. Slowly, Tony touched the kit with his hand, watching Sheba's reaction to his handling her offspring. She raised herself more comfortably, gave a deep sigh and closed her eyes. Tony picked the kit up and examined it, and found it to be male. I was out and as Tony did not want to move and so disturb Sheba, he called to our neighbour, Eddie Messer. Tony's tone was so urgent that Eddie thought there was an emergency, perhaps a fire. He came running fast into our garden to the compound. Tony did not say anything, but just smiled and pointed to mother and son on his lap. Eddie fetched a Polaroid camera and spent the next half hour photographing the scene.

When I came in, Tony asked me to bring my kitchen scales and a tape measure. The kit weighed eight and three-quarter ounces and measured ten inches. Tony held the kit up to the wire mesh and I tentatively touched him with my little finger through the wire – his fur was very fine and soft. The next day, the vet. called and Sheba quite happily allowed Tony to pick up the kit and show him to the vet., who confirmed that it was a male and very healthy.

It was a week later, after I had continually admired the kit, that Sheba allowed me to pick him up myself. As Sheba and I are normally good friends, we can only think that her initial reluctance to my touching the kit was because I am another female.

We named the kit Brutus and, when he was born, Snoopy started to keep his section very clean. Before the birth, Snoopy would kick his full toilet tray upside down or else not use it at all. Tony did not reunite Snoopy and Sheba for fear that Snoopy might eat Brutus, supposedly to bring Sheba into season again, but he watched his son and was very interested. He was shut away in the other section of the sleeping quarters and Tony had nailed a wooden board over the wire grid in the partition to ensure Sheba's complete privacy and also to prevent any possible accident if Snoopy pushed a claw through and scratched the kit.

When Brutus was born, his eyes were still closed and at twelve days they gradually opened to reveal periwinkle blue eyes; later they would change to brown. Sheba was a good mother and very protective towards Brutus. He was adventurous and if he strayed too far from her box, Sheba would haul him back. Brutus soon discovered the tree trunks in the compound and even at an early age tried to climb them.

As Brutus grew older, Sheba gradually began to push him away from her, especially when he became too rough, when she would snap at him which she had not done before. We thought it best to have Brutus in the house, so we brought him in, for longer periods each time, until eventually he stayed permanently with us and Snoopy and Sheba were together again.

Chapter Six

Living with an ocelot is like living with a child who never grows up. As a kit, Snoopy was quiet, probably because we were not the first owners he had, and exotic cats hate change of ownership. Brutus was boisterous and rough and what was once an appealing and harmless kit with spotted fur, grew into a cat with powerful teeth, razor sharp claws, solid muscles and frequently a strong will of its own. Happily, we were fairly successful in teaching young Brutus not to use his teeth and claws too hard or too often on humans. He was never vicious and if he did bite and draw blood, it was an accident. He could be rough though and sometimes his teeth pinched me so hard that my skin was bruised. I would then speak sharply to him, he would relax his grip, but to make him let go entirely, I would have to distract him, usually by throwing a suitable handy object for him to chase. If there was no such object readily available, I would usually resort to slipping off my shoe and kicking it high into the air and then watch, with admiration, Brutus leaping in one liquid, flowing movement to catch the shoe with mouth and paws; then he would immediately throw it up in the air again and spring, from a standing position, to catch it in mid-air.

Poppet's temperament was different from that of Brutus. Being female, she was naturally quieter than he and, being heavier, she did not have the same 'spring' that he had. It has been said that ocelots have a 'Napoleon complex', that being so small they tend to be aggressive to compensate for their size. Poppet did not have this complex being so much larger and stronger.

At two months, Brutus was little different from a domestic kitten, but soon we noticed the gradual changes. His muscles were becoming strong and hard to the touch; his eyes changed from their baby blue to deep chocolate brown; he always seemed to be climbing – up trouser legs, his little claws, like sharp needles, pricking one through the cloth. Once, he climbed into the empty grate and up the chimney.

I had shut him in the lounge while answering the telephone and on returning, could not see him. I knew that he must be in the room as no window or door had been left open and yet I could not find him. Then I heard a plaintive cry, not exactly a mew, but a deeper jungle sound, coming from the chimney. I looked up the chimney and there, a little way up on a ledge, was a black, fluffy object, the only part of which that was not black was its mouth which kept opening to show a pink tongue and white teeth as it cried.

I put my arm up the chimney and soot fell down the wide sleeves of my dress. As I placed my hand round him to lift him down, Brutus, in fright, jabbed all his claws into my arm, as if it were a pin cushion, and clung to me. I quickly brought the frightened kit down the chimney, gently placed him on the carpet and unhooked his inbedded claws from my arm. He scampered away leaving a sooty trail and I bandaged my arm thinking of the exotic cat owners' adage that if one were afraid of being clawed, one should not keep these cats.

One room had to be set aside especially for Brutus and our ornaments were gradually placed higher and higher out of his reach until it was necessary to remove them altogether. By this time, Willy Domestic Cat was very staid and successfully kept out of the new rough kit's way. Occasionally there was a confrontation between them, when Willy stood on her dignity with one paw raised, which perhaps brought back memories of Sheba to Brutus for he scampered away, wisely rejecting Willy as a plaything.

Although Brutus has a will of his own, he is also obedient. When still a kit he began to sharpen his claws on the furniture and carpets, but stopped after I had firmly told him not to, using instead the scratching post which I hurriedly bought. If there was danger and he was told, sternly, to stay still, he did so. As we could not hide every electric wire in the house, we taught him not to touch them until, eventually, he just ignored them. We do, however, take the precaution of switching off the electric current if we leave him alone in a room for any length of time.

As Brutus was a single animal without a companion, we wanted to avoid his becoming bored so I bought an old scooter tyre, washed it and then hung it from a ceiling beam as a swing for him. He spent many hours playing, swinging backwards and forwards, jumping through it to perform graceful acrobatics and somersaults, worrying it and eventually climbing up the rope on to the ceiling beam. However, he was not able to slide down the rope again and cried pitifully to be lifted down – his bravado gone.

Like his mother, Sheba, Brutus was, and still is, very affectionate. As a kit living with us, he insisted, first thing every morning, on licking and nuzzling our faces, purring loudly all the time. He then pushed his nose under the bedclothes, wriggled underneath and rushed to the bottom of the bed to mock attack our bare toes.

I find that I have more affinity with him, being male, than Tony has. Whenever I cup his face in my hands and kiss his nose repeatedly, he makes a deep-throated, continuous purring sound, then winds himself, like a whirling hoop, round and round me for several minutes. He then becomes too excited and starts to nip my legs and thighs hard until I distract him with a favourite toy.

I made Brutus a rag doll out of an old woollen dress and was careful to stuff it with natural fibres, which would not hurt him if he swallowed them. Still very young, he took his rag doll everywhere with him and would not settle down for the night until it was tucked underneath him. He would delight in dropping the doll into the toilet to swish it around in the water. Once, he was too enthusiastic and slipped head first into the pan, wedging half way. I heard an urgent yowling and rushed into the bathroom to see just his legs and tail sticking out over the side. It was a wet and subdued cat which was pulled out to be dried and comforted. Eventually, Brutus learnt to lift the toilet cover himself and so the toilet was placed out of bounds for him by keeping the door locked.

Ocelots are notorious for being able to open doors and drawers and Brutus was no exception. Some doors had to be kept locked because, as he grew older, he soon learnt that if he jumped up at a door handle and pulled it down, the door would open. Eventually we had to change some door handles for knobs which Brutus could not turn. He also learnt to open drawers and found it great fun to pull a drawer out and then to spring backwards out of the way as the contents tumbled on to the floor and then he would kick them around the room. One desk which could not be locked had to be turned round, with its front facing the wall away from him after he had pulled the drawers out several times. I had a splendid rubber plant, with large, glossy leaves until Brutus discovered it and systematically removed the foliage. I found it with just the stem sticking out of the pot and Brutus playing with the remains of the leaves.

Brutus delights in springing on to his friends' shoulders, suddenly if possible, to startle them. If he is caught out just as he is about to spring, he looks disconcerted and pretends to be engrossed in other things, like pouncing, unexpectedly, at passing legs and then racing away to skid to a halt when he is out of the reach of the molested human.

I bought him a ball made from solid rubber, but took the precaution of never leaving it with him knowing how sharp his teeth were, in case he managed to chew and swallow pieces of it, with possibly fatal results. He learnt to retrieve the ball quickly for it to be thrown again and this kept him, and us, amused for hours. Like Poppet Leopard, he would take potatoes from the kitchen to play with and would, on occasions, retrieve these, though he preferred the bouncing ball, which he would spring to catch in mid-air. As his father, when a kit, had liked to play with hard-boiled eggs and carrots, I gave these to Brutus also, but he would soon crunch them, become bored and leave the pieces scattered over a wide area.

Another favourite toy which delighted him but which he had difficulty in getting under my eagle eye, was a rubber hot-water bottle. He would attack and worry it until the water spurted out, like a fountain, usually on to the bed. Not infrequently, I would suddenly realise that Brutus was too quiet, and on investigating, would find him relaxing on the bed, looking contented, his front paws on the torn remains of the hot-water bottle, the water from which having already soaked into the bedclothes. Then, I would scold him, snatch the torn bottle away, still dripping, whereupon he would usually roll over on his back and gently smack me playfully with his paws, his claws sheathed.

As all the cats enjoy cooked chicken and turkey, I choose a slightly larger bird than I would normally for the family, so that the cats can have some too, as a change from their normal meat. I have to be careful to remove all the bones first for them, because cooked bones would splinter and could cause internal injury. Snoopy relishes smoked salmon, and has it as an occasional treat. Fortunately he is the only cat that does! I am relieved that Poppet Leopard dislikes it otherwise I can imagine her eating a whole side of expensive smoked salmon in one gulp. Like Snoopy, Brutus enjoys cottage cheese, but only the plain variety, and thought apples were splendid toys to be tossed around until he found them good to eat as well.

When Tony has a headache, he obtains relief if I pull his hair hard. Brutus must have watched me do this because one day, when Tony was sitting in a chair, Brutus jumped up behind him, put his front paws on to his shoulders, took a mouthful of hair and tugged. As Tony did not chase him away, he continued until he had pulled at every hair, dribbling whilst he was doing it, so that Tony's hair and scalp were damp with saliva. Inexplicably, Brutus enjoys pulling human hair and it is sometimes difficult to remove him from Tony's shoulders. One day, some friends called and while the man was talking to Tony, his wife sat on the sofa with me. After a few minutes, I went into the kitchen to make some coffee, leaving her reading a magazine. Suddenly there was an urgent shriek from the girl and the next moment, Brutus came bounding into the kitchen with what looked like a lump of hair in his mouth. He was closely followed by the girl crying in an unusually high-pitched voice, "He's got my wig!"

Apparently, Brutus had jumped onto the back of the sofa and had started to pull at her hair, as usual, which came away in his mouth. I quickly snatched a piece of meat to try to distract him so that I could rescue the wig, but he raced out of the kitchen, skilfully avoiding our outstretched hands. He tripped over the wig, part of which had fallen out of his mouth and was trailing on the ground, which gave me time to catch up with him. He then began shaking and tossing the wig up in the air, but always catching it before me to streak away again out of my reach. Tony returned and between us we managed to retrieve the tangled mess of hair, which was once a wig, by giving him a pink feather duster to play with instead. He was shut away in another room while we placated the girl and I made arrangements to buy her a replacement wig. When I looked in on Brutus, some time later, he was sleeping peacefully on a cushion, exhausted by his riotous morning and surrounded by pink feathers.

All the cats have their own blankets and when my ancient washing machine is unable to cope, I take them to a launderette. The combination of leopard and oceolot smell is distinctive and the other customers look puzzled and their noses twitch when I walk in carrying the soiled blankets. The cats tear their blankets and the launderette customers look surprised as I fold neatly, newly washed blankets, some of which are badly torn. On one occasion, the launderette machine broke down just after I had put in a particularly smelly load of animal blankets. I had left the launderette to go to other shops and on returning found that the dragon-like lady in charge had yanked out the sodden blankets with their distinctive odour, and put them into a basket. She said, her voice rising. "These smell dreadful, have monkeys been using them?" I thought if I told her that a leopard, ocelots and a fox had lain on them, she would have an apoplectic fit. Fortunately, the worst blankets were in another machine which was working properly. From lack of courage, I told her, on the spur of the moment, and being unable to think of anything else, that my husband had taken them camping. She wanted to know what he was doing to get them in such a state and I could see that her mind was boggling. I told her that I did not know as I did not go with him and my lie was corroborated by an old pair of men's pants and vest which I had given one of the animals as additional bedding. She obviously did not believe my transparent lie, because I was told not to bring such dreadful washing into her launderette again. I have not been drummed out of any other similar establishment, but I do avoid the one which has a notice on its wall 'Clean washing only'. I often wonder if they mean that 'ordinary' clothes should be washed at home first. As I was obviously being unfair to other launderette users, I bought a secondhand washing machine exclusively for the animals' bedding.

When Brutus was five months old, Tony was told that H.M.S. *Ocelot* was being recommissioned in Scotland and that the captain would like Snoopy, their mascot, to be present at the Re-Commissioning Ceremony. As Brutus was an extrovert and liked human company, we decided to take him as a substitute mascot instead of his father. Since becoming adult, and being with Sheba, Snoopy has become unpredictable with humans, especially males, possibly because he is protecting his female as he is all right with me.

We had planned to travel to Scotland by train, but the day before the ceremony we heard that there was to be a rail strike the next day. Tony had already alerted the *Daily Express* that we were taking Brutus since this newspaper had followed our ocelot story from the beginning. He then had to telephone the paper to say that we would be unable to reach Scotland the next day as he had been told that all the airline seats were fully booked because of the rail strike. However, the *Daily Express* came to the rescue and were able to arrange to fly not only Tony, Brutus and myself to Edinburgh, but also the wife of the captain of H.M.S. *Ocelot*, who had been stranded in London.

Brutus, in his blue carrying box, travelled as cargo and as we disembarked first, we waited for him in the arrival lounge at Edinburgh Airport. Tony was the first to see the blue box trundling along the luggage conveyor belt, with Brutus looking out through the wire mesh at the front.

When Tony lifted the box off the belt, he was surprised to find that it was very cold. We opened it, Brutus rubbed himself against Tony's hand and licked him and seemed to be all right, but we were, of course, concerned about the low temperature in which he had travelled. The Navy cars however were waiting and as Brutus seemed to be none the worse after the flight, we set off towards H.M.S. *Ocelot.*

As we walked towards the submarine, there was a gale-force wind blowing and I had to cling to one roped side of the gangplank. I quickly reached the conning-tower and held on to it tightly as the wind fiercely whipped my clothes. I was helped on board, followed by Tony carrying Brutus in his blue box. Brutus behaved well for the photographers and we all went ashore and made him comfortable in one of the officer's cabins.

That evening, Tony and I, together with Brutus, went to the Commissioning Ceremony, which was a new experience for all of us. It was held in what seemed to be, in the January darkness, a large drill hall in the dockyard. A Royal Marine band, dressed magnificently, were playing splendidly. The captain read the Commissioning Warrant, the ensign was hoisted and the masthead pendant broken. After the Act of Dedication, the captain called on the ship's company to ask for God's blessing on the ship, using a Gaelic blessing of 1589. When the ceremony was over the captain's wife cut the commissioning cake and Brutus made for a grand piano in a corner, jumped onto it and stretched out elegantly to be admired.

There was a lady at the ceremony wearing an ocelot jacket, made from jungle ocelots' skins, the same colouring as Brutus. Tony did not allow Brutus to go near the ocelot coat in case he tore it thinking it was alive. I looked at the coat and felt very sad as I knew that at least seven ocelots had been killed to make this lady's waist-length fur jacket and that her coat could arouse in others the desire to own a similar garment – more animals killed by man not for meat but solely for profit.

Each ocelot skin nets about £30 to the hunters of Peru, which is the equivalent of three or four hard days' work for gold. The traps are made from logs which are fashioned into a sort of cage and a dead monkey is placed inside as bait. When the ocelot tries to grab the bait the rope supporting the logs serves as a trapdoor snaps loose and the logs come down trapping the animal inside the cage. The ocelot is then killed by strangulation by the hunter so as not to damage its coat.

Eventually, it was time to go in order to catch our plane back to London. At the airport, Tony asked to see the controller to complain about Brutus' cold carrying case on the outward flight. The British Airways controller was very helpful and as the homeward plane was almost empty, he put us and Brutus, much to our relief, in a compartment to ourselves at the back of the plane. Brutus, in his box, was placed on a seat and the safety belt fastened round the box. The air hostesses made a fuss of him and found some cooked chicken left over from lunch and gave him that – we had coffee and biscuits!

This was the first time that Brutus had been away from his home and he seemed pleased, or relieved, to be back because that night he was so good, rubbing himself against us and purring and not nipping, that we let him sleep with us. The following morning he was still good, but by evening he was again his usual rough self giving 'beatings up' and nips and crunches with his sharp teeth.

Tony had built a large enclosure for Brutus in the garden, with tree trunks and grass and wooden sleeping quarters. After living in the house, Brutus was nervous of being in the wide open space outdoors and stayed in his sleeping quarters for most of the first few days, but soon began to venture into the enclosure. I fixed his rubber tyre onto a rope in the centre of the run so that he would have a familiar object with which to play. Tony brought him back into the house every couple of days, which we have continued to do ever since and he, and other animals, take it in turns to be with us.

Once, while Snoopy was with us in the house, we put Sheba in with Brutus for company. We are sure that Sheba recognised her son, even though she had not seen him for some months. She licked him and afterwards watched him with a soft expression in her eyes. Later, they shared the same blanket and slept curled round one another.

A few days later, there was an accident and Brutus was inadvertently bitten on the foot by Sheba. I was in the compound feeding them and gave Brutus, who was nearest me, a piece of meat. I was just about to give Sheba some when Tony called me and I left the enclosure. As I turned to fasten the door, I happened to glance at the two ocelots and saw that Brutus had his paw on his piece of meat his claws digging into it firmly. Sheba tried, unsuccessfully, to pull the meat away, tried again and in so doing, her teeth caught Brutus' paw. Brutus removed his paw from the meat and Sheba snatched it and rushed inside the sleeping quarters with it. I ran back to give Brutus another piece of meat and saw that his paw was bleeding and when Tony, who had come into the garden, examined it he saw that a toe was badly torn.

I fetched the portable cage and we coaxed Brutus inside and carried him into the house. Tony telephoned our animals' vet. at his home as it was past surgery hours but the vet. was unable to come as he was just on his way to a farm to perform an operation on a cow. He told Tony that he considered him perfectly capable of stitching the paw provided we took Brutus to his surgery that evening so that Tony's handiwork could be checked. A few weeks previously Tony had completed a course at the Royal

College of Veterinary Surgeons which had included suturing techniques.

With the vet.'s approval, Tony used Acetylpromazine in tablet form and injections to tranquillise Brutus deeply. He crushed half tablets into fine powder and placed inside pieces of meat and gave them to the injured cat; about an hour and a half passed before Brutus was practically 'unconscious'. As these exotic cats are highly susceptible to death by anaesthetic Tony considers it safer to tranquillise them slowly rather than by one big shot.

While Brutus was gradually becoming tranquillised, Tony decided to use the top of the deep freeze as an operating table as it is the only large surface in the kitchen. I lifted Handsome Parrot in his cage from the kitchen into the bathroom and shooed Willy Domestic Cat, who had been snoozing in a corner, outside. I scrubbed the freezer lid, disinfected it and Tony laid out his instruments. By this time, Brutus was staggering, his legs looked as if they were made of thin rubber so we stayed close by him so that he did not fall and hurt himself further. I sat on the floor with him and in the final stages or excitement period, just before Brutus became immobile, he rubbed himself violently over my legs and began to bite me hard but Tony came to my rescue and distracted him.

At last he was under sedation and Tony carefully lifted him up on to the freezer top and on examination found a three-inch rip on his right foreleg exposing the bone and part of the tendon. One toe had practically been severed and was only attached by a minute piece of skin. Tony cleaned and stitched the major wound and then turned his attention to the toe which, due to the lack of blood flow, would have eventually dropped off. Tony decided to try to save it and after shaving the surrounding fur, stitched the toe to the foot using nine stitches.

As Tony had only used the minimum of tranquilliser

required, Brutus was only just under the surface of 'unconsciousness' and my job was to hold him. Another of my duties was to mop Tony's brow while he was stitching. At last, the operation was finished just before Brutus regained consciousness.

Tony placed Brutus inside a carrying box to avoid weight being placed on the injured toe and to keep him warm. That evening, the vet. examined Brutus' paw and said that Tony's stitching was satisfactory. During the following weeks, the paw healed well and today there are no visible signs of any injury and Brutus is walking perfectly on that foot.

Fortunately, I have a happier relationship with Brutus Ocelot than with Poppet Leopard. A few weeks ago, Tony and I went inside Brutus' enclosure and he wound himself round and round us, excited to see us. Then he started to concentrate on me and eventually dug his teeth hard into my thigh. As he did not touch Tony, we assumed that this was a sexual movement. Obviously, it was getting near the time for Brutus to have a female companion and to this end, Tony has been granted an Import Licence for two female ocelots either domestic born or zoo bred as it is against our principles to be responsible for these creatures being taken from the wild.

Chapter Seven

Last Easter, there was a knock on the front door. I opened it to find a neighbour who told me that there was a sick fox in his garden. I called Tony, and together we ran about half a mile to the garden and there, on a concrete path, was a fox, completely motionless, which could only have been about two weeks old. Tony gently and carefully picked up the cub and examined it. The animal's eyes were closed and it was hardly breathing. He thought it probably had pneumonia. The tiny creature's fur was wet and caked with mud and it felt as cold as marble. Tony undid his jacket and placed the fox cub inside, holding it close to the warmth of his body. We slowly started to walk home, stopping often to make sure that the cub, a male, was still breathing; its eyes remained tightly shut.

At home, I warmed some milk, into which Tony put a few drops of brandy and with which he filled a syringe. He lifted the fox's head and gently placed the nozzle of the syringe into its mouth. As the liquid trickled down its throat, the cub's eyes began to flicker for a few moments and then closed again. Tony tenderly massaged the tiny pathetic animal, again holding it close to him hoping that the warmth from his body would penetrate the fur.

After a few minutes, the cub's eyes gradually opened and we could see that one eye had a squint and was very watery. Tony then filled the syringe with chicken essence and the cub started, weakly and hesitantly at first, to lick the nozzle. We refilled the syringe and this time, the baby fox held on to the nozzle with his teeth. When he had finished we wrapped him in a blanket and placed him in a cardboard box in a warm place out of the draught. The fox gave a deep sigh and went to sleep, but this time his breathing was much stronger.

We wondered what to call him and as one of the first things I had noticed about the cub was that he smelt strongly, we decided on Stinky. Throughout the day, we kept a careful watch on him, giving him more chicken essence with the syringe, which he now greedily started to gulp, pulling at the nozzle so firmly that I had to keep a tight grip on it.

The next morning, I awoke at about six o'clock and quietly crept over to the cardboard box, looked inside and, with relief, saw that the fox was still breathing. I hesitantly reached out and stroked the reddish brown fur and at my touch the cub stirred, made a tiny whimpering sound, then snuggled down into the blankets and went back to sleep – and so did I.

Later that day, I met one of our neighbours on the island and told her about finding the fox. She told me that when she had been exercising her dog two evenings previously, it had run up to an animal with reddish brown fur, lying still on the ground. She had not investigated thinking it was a dying cat, nor had she told anyone who might have been able to help the creature. I showed her the fox and she said she was certain that it was the same animal which her dog had found. We remembered that particular night had been cold and so the fox must have struggled from where the dog had found it, across the road and the many hundreds of yards to the garden.

During the days that followed Tony and I went to the field to the warren to look for any other lone cubs, but could not find any. Stinky gradually became stronger until he was able to feed himself and to stagger slowly, on uncertain legs, out of his cardboard box, one side of which we had cut away so that he could easily climb in and out and around the room if he wished.

A few nights later, we were driving home when the car's headlights picked out two foxes in the road. I instantly stopped the car, one fox ran away but the other stood still for a few moments until Tony had almost reached it. It tried to run away but was too weak, so Tony picked it up and placed it in the car. It was about the same size as Stinky, but much thinner and its eyes had shrunk into its head. It was having difficulty in breathing and kept opening its mouth silently. Tony said he thought it had been poisoned. When we reached home, we tried to feed it with milk and brandy in a syringe as we had done with Stinky, but it would not swallow. Tony administered an emetic to try to save it and saw that its mouth was burnt and ulcerated. The next morning it was dead. For several days, we put food out for the other fox cub that had run away, but the food remained untouched.

Unfortunately, the squint in Stinky's left eye was so bad that he did not always see the food when it was placed in front of him and he was always bumping into furniture. With our vet.'s approval, Tony placed some eye ointment into Stinky's squint eye, and into the other one as well in case that was infected. As he could not see to fend for himself, we did not want to turn him loose in the wild and, after much discussion, we felt that we should keep him, at least for a time, hoping that his sight would improve when we could then release him. We could not bear the thought of Stinky being hunted, whimpering with terror. We appreciate that foxes can do a great deal of damage and that farmers must protect their livestock by killing them, but we hope it is always done humanely – we think of the agony of

Snoopy joins the navy – on board H.M.S. Ocelot
(*Crown copyright – Royal Navy Photograph*)

Fred shows off his 'trousers' (*Copyright Colin Browne*)

Baby Fox and Wilhelmenia – a truce (*Copyright Tony Travers*)

Sheba entrusts the newly born Brutus to Tony
(*Copyright Daily Telegraph*)

Sheba takes a cat-nap (*Copyright Tony Travers*)

Three-legged Poppet gazes lovingly at Tony (*Copyright Tony Travers*)

Cleo at play (*Copyright Tony Travers*)

Cleo – the cat who got the cream (*Copyright Tony Travers*)

the poisoned fox we found. About that time, I watched a discussion on television on fox hunting, both for and against, and I was horrified to hear one of the hunters say that he hunts foxes for *fun*. When Tony and I went to the field to try to find Stinky's brothers, we found the remains of wood pigeons near the warren, so surely, in that instance, the fox was helping the farmer by killing the pigeons which were eating his corn.

One day, Stinky made a tiny darting movement at my hand, gave it a gentle nip before immediately running away and squinting at me from behind a chair. I got down on the carpet on all fours, whereupon Stinky ran towards me, touched me with his wet nose and then raced off again. We played like this for some time, until he flopped down and went to sleep.

When he was completely better, except for his poor eyesight, Tony put Stinky into the kitchen sink and carefully poured luke warm water on to his body only, not his head, and gently, using a baby shampoo, lathered and rinsed him. We dried him with an old towel and let him race around the house to finish drying. We found that the fox did not respond to the name Stinky and when he was tiny I often called him Baby Fox. It was this name that he began to know as his and as he no longer smelt after shampooing, we changed his name officially to Baby Fox. I think it is the 'b-b' of 'baby' he recognises.

Unhappily, I was unsuccessful in house training Baby Fox. He rarely used exactly the same spot twice. Directly I saw him urinating, I would rush and put down newspaper, which he immediately started to play with, tearing it to pieces. I bought special liquid from the pet shop which is supposed to encourage kittens and puppies to be house trained, but this had no effect at all. As the smell of a fox's urine is strong and offensive, Tony built a run, complete with a kennel, for Baby Fox in the garden and we brought him into the house for several hours play every evening as he slept during the day.

It so happened that we were unable to have him in the house for three consecutive evenings and when Baby Fox came into the house on the fourth evening, we found that we had lost mental contact with him. He did not want to know us, he was frightened and ran around the room whimpering, which rose in volume every time we went near him. It took until the early hours of the morning to gradually win his confidence until he was playing and nuzzling us again as usual. We kept him in the house for the rest of the night. Baby Fox disliked being picked up to be petted and would jump out of our arms as soon as he could and would immediately shake himself.

One morning, some weeks later, Baby Fox was very sick. Tony brought him into the house and placed him on our bed. I mixed Terramycetin powder in water, which he drank. We kept him warm, gave him some more of the Terramycetin all that day and by the evening he was a little better. Tony thinks that his illness was caused by eating some rotten meat which he had, like all foxes, buried some time before, presumably as emergency supplies.

During my efforts to house train Baby Fox, I had bought a large sheet of blotting paper, white so that he could see it easily. After yet one more smelly mishap some weeks previously, I had soaked the blotting paper in his urine and left it in the garden to dry. As he would obviously have to stay in the house until he was better, I fetched the impregnated blotting paper. Baby Fox was lying on our bed, his eyes open watching me, but he did not raise his head at my approach. I put the blotting paper under his nose so that he could smell that it was 'his' and told him very firmly, to pee on it. I then put the blotting paper down in a corner of the bedroom which I thought he might use. But I was wrong. Baby Fox went outside our bedroom to a dark corner in the adjoining passage to wet. After I had once more mopped up the puddle, I put the dried blotting paper there and from then on, much to my immense relief, he used that as his 'toilet'. When I ran out of blotting paper, I put newspaper down in that corner, which he used and has continued to do ever since. He never tears his 'toilet' newspaper to shreds, though he will tear other newspaper – especially the current daily paper.

Now that Baby Fox is house trained, he spends a great deal of time in the house. As he is a nocturnal animal, I have to shut him in the bathroom at night otherwise we would not have any sleep – it is still winter and too cold to put him in the outdoors run. Sometimes, he scratches and shakes the door to be let in from the bathroom, and if we do so towards dawn, he will very often crawl under our bed to sleep for about an hour and then will leap on the bed and jump on us, to wake us, to play with him. During the day, he sleeps in our bedroom, either on the bed or against the hot radiator.

Baby Fox is still not keen on being picked up, though he does not now shake himself on being released as he once did before his illness. Tony and I can stroke him without his automatically dashing away and when we do so, and if he is in the mood, he purrs, and rubs himself against us like a cat but he hates his brush being touched and whimpers if anyone does so.

When Baby Fox is given food and is not hungry, he hides it around the house, mainly in corners, but if he decides to secrete titbits under a carpet, he always pulls it back again so that his food is completely hidden, except for the tell-tale bump. He is very fond of Irish stew and I have to watch very carefully to see under which carpets he hides his emergency supplies of that. After he has gone to sleep in the mornings, I meticulously remove his hidden food to avoid it going rotten with a possible recurrence of his illness.

Part of his play pattern is to grip one's clothing in his sharp teeth, then tug continuously, bouncing up and down at each tug. He will do this for several minutes and I either have to walk slowly, with a fox tugging my trousers in the opposite direction, or rub his nose to make him release me. This was very embarrassing on one occasion when our local V.A.T. inspectors, a man and a woman, arrived together with our accountant, to inspect Tony's books. They had all called by appointment as we keep our garden gate permanently locked because of the animals, which the V.A.T. inspectors told me afterwards they thought were dogs!

I made morning coffee and began to carry the heavy tray in to them. Just as I opened the door, Baby Fox rushed forward and snatched at my trousers and tugged, jumping with excitement. I froze, not wanting to spill the coffee, but he pulled so hard that I had no alternative but to shuffle backwards with him. The V.A.T. inspectors looked up but could not see the fox and so naturally wondered why I was hovering in the doorway for a few moments, then going backwards taking their coffee away from them, with a pained expression on my face as Baby Fox had inadvertently nipped my ankle.

I called to Tony to take the tray and when he had done so, I slowly walked into the office dragging Baby Fox like a ball and chain to show them what had been keeping me. The inspectors and the accountant burst out laughing and Baby Fox was so surprised at the new sound that he let go of my trousers and inquisitively rushed round them to investigate, so we took the opportunity to chase him out of the room.

While Baby Fox is fairly rough with human feet, legs and hands, he is always very gentle with the human face, usually rubbing his wet nose against one's cheek. I bought him a multi-coloured ball, hoping that he would find it easier to focus on with his squint, and he played with this each day until he became bored with it. He prefers to nip ankles to playing with his ball, as they move and their owners shriek. When we first took him in and before we had taught him after his illness not to nip so hard, I had to wear wellington boots indoors or else sit with my legs high in the air out of the reach of his needle sharp teeth.

One day, during the summer, Tony and I arranged to visit some friends in Sussex whose small son was convalescing after an operation. They suggested that as their son was becoming bored and fractious after so long in bed, that Baby Fox might help considerably in amusing him. We agreed, and as we had some photographs of our animals for the editor of the R.S.P.C.A.'s journal, we could deliver them personally as their office headquarters at Horsham were on the way to our friends.

I had never been to the R.S.P.C.A.'s headquarters before and my first impression as we drove in was of a large building. I told Tony that it looked rather grand for a charity, but he told me to wait until I was inside and I would see the economies. It was not a modern office block, but a fairly old building, originally a private house and then a school, which had been converted into offices. Those offices which Tony had seen were small and few people had an office to themselves. The rent from their old headquarters in London probably pays for them. We went inside, and I saw vinyl on the floors, no carpets, and on the telephones were stickers 'It's cheaper after 12'. Tony delivered the photographs to the editor, Thelma How, and happened to mention that we had a fox in our car. The editor said that she would like to see him, so Tony carried Baby Fox in his arms and placed him on the floor in the editor's office. Baby Fox darted around, peered into the wastepaper bin, knocked it over, scattering the papers over the floor, then bounded up onto the desk, skidded over some papers and jumped to the floor. As the small office was becoming too crowded for three humans and one energetic fox, we opened the door to the larger general office where several people were working. Baby Fox ran around and saw a girl secretary wearing a pair of bright yellow shoes. He rushed up to her, nipped her ankles and started tugging excitedly at the shoe laces, dancing up and down. I quickly scooped him up into my arms and Thelma How said she thought some other people would like to see him. She took us into the Press Office shared by two people, the only place for their filing cabinets was the corridor, where Baby Fox was admired. His brush, by that time, was thick and bushy, his coat, which I had brushed that morning, gleamed and his squint eye was not watering that day. Baby Fox struggled to be put down but as both Tony and I had visions of him wrecking yet another office, we left hurriedly.

At our friends' house, Baby Fox was placed on the sick child's bed. I raised my index finger to him and told him sternly to be gentle. He had, by that time, begun to realise that my raised index finger, together with a stern tone of voice, meant that he had to behave; and he did. Foxes are naturally intelligent and Baby Fox seemed to know that the child was ill because he treated him gently, nuzzling him with his button nose and gently romping over the bed until the boy fell asleep and Baby Fox snoozed too.

The next day, Brutus was out in his enclosure; the day was dull and overcast and towards afternoon the rain came. As there is a roof over part of his enclosure, Brutus does not normally become very wet, though like all of his kind, he enjoys water. But that day, his tail somehow became soaked. The rest of his body was dry and knowing Brutus, he probably deliberately dipped it into a puddle and swished it around so that he could play with the water. His tail was bedraggled with the water and consequently thin, like a rat's, and because it had lost its familiar fat and bushy shape, Brutus could not have recognised it as his. He started to chase it fast like a spinning top. We have never seen him chase his tail when it is dry and its normal shape. I tried to distract him by offering him his favourite titbit but he ignored me and continued whizzing round until he stopped from tiredness.

Brutus is a very fine specimen, taller and longer than his father and mother but Snoopy is a little broader than his son though doubtless, in time, Brutus will broaden as well. Brutus' tail is very strong and thick, whereas Snoopy's is slender in comparison, whilst Sheba's tail is pathetically thin. We have often read about the long legged ocelot and that is Brutus; his parents' legs are much shorter and stubbier.

Day by day, Baby Fox grew stronger, more mischievous, and affectionate. I let him into our bedroom first thing every morning while Tony is in bed smoking. He is fascinated by this and at first, after watching Tony lighting cigarettes several times, pounced on the cigarette packet and ran off with it. By the time I had retrieved it, the cigarettes were punctured by his teeth, sharp like daggers. After that, Tony, while in bed, would hide the cigarette packet underneath the pillow when Baby Fox was occupied elsewhere. A few mornings later, Baby Fox saw where Tony had hidden the cigarette packet and suddenly dived under the pillow, pulled the packet out and before Tony could stop him, raced away. Tony then had to guard his cigarettes and Baby Fox was unsuccessful in getting them until one morning, he feigned an attack on Tony's hand and while Tony's attention was distracted, snatched the packet from under the pillow. This time, Tony was too quick for him and rescued the packet which is now placed on a shelf too high for the fox to reach. When Tony is sitting down relaxing, his attention elsewhere, Baby Fox will surreptitiously poke his long nose into Tony's jacket pockets but usually not quietly enough.

One evening just before Baby Fox was due to wake up at ten o'clock, there were some dogs on the television barking furiously and their noise woke him. He looked enquiringly at the television and then at me – his squint eye was markedly askew. I reassured him and he went back to sleep, but I saw fear momentarily in his eyes and as the only dog he had met was plump, soft Jester, the dachshund from next door with whom he is friends, I wondered if his fear of his kind being hunted by dogs had been inbred over the centuries.

Tony and I find it is important to Baby Fox to play with him each evening; if we gently hold the root of his brush, he will run round in a tight circle and we can spin him like a top for a few seconds. He enjoys playing with my slippers, worrying and shaking them and throwing them up in the air, and if he can, he will remove them from my feet. He has two ticklish spots in the centre of his back and if we press them, he stands still, his head goes down and he snorts with pleasure for a few moments before racing round the room again to suddenly dart and nip our ankles.

Another fox game is to take things from the bathroom and kitchen, race into the bedroom and deposit them on the bed. I have found my hairbrush; the bathroom loose mat (a favourite); a plastic bag containing the remains of a roll of cotton wool, the rest of which was strewn, like a paper chase, between the bathroom and the bedroom; a piece of fillet steak from the shopping I had just bought and also potatoes. He is fascinated by the kitchen refuse bin and he soon learnt to ram his long nose under the lid and lift. After being scolded many times, he does not normally rummage in the bin, but just contents himself with sniffing round it eagerly though occasionally he forgets and I find soggy, discarded tea bags and other kitchen refuse on our bed. Once, when the refuse bin was full and before I had time to empty it, I had absent-mindedly put an old packet of cream crackers, now soft, beside the bin to be thrown away. Baby Fox found them, picked them up and rushed, as usual, into the bedroom, where he tore the wrapping off and threw the biscuits around, gambolling like a lamb.

One morning, I gave Baby Fox a piece of meat. He raced into the bedroom but inadvertently dropped it behind the bed. He tried to retrieve it, but could not, so he ran back to me whimpering and continued to whimper until I had recovered the meat and given it back to him.

Baby Fox is easy to feed. He has meat like the cats and also cheese, chocolate pudding and almost everything else that is going. He is especially fond of raiding Willy Domestic Cat's food dish. If Willy is there, she stands back, looking indignant, her fur beginning to rise, as she watches him at her dish but as a rule I shut the fox out of the kitchen while giving Willy her food.

When Baby Fox first came into the house, Willy ignored him until he nipped her tail, whereupon she turned and smacked him with her paw. If he became too familiar with her, she made a high pitched whining sound and raised her paw to strike, though she rarely did because Baby Fox usually sniffed once, then backed and ran away. Nowadays, they are used to one another, especially after having had to share a bed in the floods which were to come a few months later.

Part of Baby Fox's 'tour of inspection' when he races round the house first thing in the morning is to jump up beside Handsome Parrot's cage. Tony and I thought that Handsome would peck Baby Fox when he pushed his nose too near the parrot's cage, but this is not the case. We have both, at different times, seen them nose to beak, neither making any attempts to be aggressive. I think that sometimes Baby Fox jumps up besides Handsome's cage out of devilment because if he does so too rapidly, there is always a flapping of wings and Handsome squawks as he is startled.

One 'toy' which Baby Fox relishes is my handbag which he drags around, especially if I have forgetfully left it open. I came in one day to find my red diary in the passage, my lipstick case crunched, with the remains of the lipstick round Baby Fox's mouth, money over the floor and bank notes chewed. I managed to salvage most of the pieces of bank notes and mended them with sellotape but decided to pay them into the bank rather than try to use them as legal tender in shops, which I did not think would accept them as so many parts were missing. The bank cashier took a tattered note by the corner, held it up, looked at me and asked what had happened to it. I do not think she believed me when I told her a fox chewed them and she probably would have believed me even less if Poppet Leopard had been the culprit!

The only time when Baby Fox has bitten me and drawn blood was by accident. I had inadvertently stood on his foot for several moments, thinking I was standing on an electric wire which we had hidden under the rug. Baby Fox gave a cry which Tony and I had never heard him use before or since, it was a deep almost spine-chilling sound, which I can only describe as a 'cry of the wild', as he dug his teeth into my leg to make me move off his foot. I bled and after Tony had managed to stop the bleeding, we could see the mark of his fangs in my flesh.

I am always very unhappy to hear that fox cubs are offered for sale as pets and after a year's experience of keeping one, I wonder if these animals are suitable for the average family. Foxes have very sharp teeth and can inflict tremendous damage, both on human flesh and on property. It is extremely difficult to house train them. I had been told by a vet. and also the curator of a large zoological park that I would be unsuccessful in training Baby Fox and, even now, he sometimes urinates in unexpected places. I am sure that the average housewife does not have the time, or the energy, to do the very considerable cleaning up after a fox, continually every day, on top of her other chores. I have to clean our bathroom thoroughly every morning after Baby Fox has spent a night there running around. Foxes are nocturnal, Baby Fox sleeps from about ten in the morning to ten at night and to try to turn their clock round regularly every day is, I think, unfair to the animal.

I wonder what happens when a family decides that a pet fox is not for them. Are these unwanted foxes abandoned in the country, having been imprinted with the idea that man is their friend, unaccustomed to fending for themselves and possibly rejected by their own kind? Friends of ours took in a fox cub which had been rejected as a pet, to add to their colony of four, to prevent the local hunt from buying it – to be kept and released, in strange country, the day before the hunt.

Domestic dogs and cats can, of course, go out and meet others of their species and even if a fox is kept satisfactorily as a pet from the human point of view, is it fair to keep it singly without the companionship of its own kind? As our fox, still with limited vision, is getting older, we are starting to look for a mate for him. Knowing how animals seem to gravitate to us, I have no doubt that one day a female fox will find us.

Chapter Eight

Jo, a school teacher friend of ours, took her class to London Zoo and on returning told us that she had seen a lone ocelot there. Tony contacted the zoo, told them about our ocelots, Snoopy and Sheba, and the birth of Brutus and that he, Tony, was a member of the Zoo Federation and asked whether their ocelot was male or female. On hearing that it was female, he asked if they would agree to lend her to him to see if she would breed with Snoopy. As she was on her own, and as Snoopy had already proved himself to be fertile, London Zoo agreed to deposit her with Tony.

We went to collect her, putting a carrying box in the back of the car and taking titbits of cooked chicken. London Zoo told us that her name was Baby and that she had been presented to them nine years previously. She had had rickets when she was a kit, before she went to the zoo. On the way home in the car, Baby relaxed and seemed interested in what was going on around her. She was not nervous when a red London bus suddenly towered over the car, its engine roaring, and when we stopped at traffic lights, she peered round the corner of the box at the lighted shop windows and at the people walking by. She refused the chicken and, not surprisingly, spat whenever we put a hand near her. We talked softly to her, calling her Baby, to which she gave no sign of recognition.

We wondered how she would react to our ocelots,

especially to Snoopy, as presumably the only other ocelot she had seen had been her mother. Tony had already shut Snoopy and Sheba in one half of the sleeping quarters and, on arriving home, put Baby in the other half with the door open leaving her free to go out into the run if she wished. Baby could see Snoopy and Sheba through the wire grid in the wooden partition, but did not go up to it and remained at the far end of the sleeping quarters looking through at the other two. After a few moments, Snoopy walked slowly up to the grid and stood looking at her. Baby immediately hurried to the grid and sniffed Snoopy through it, but Snoopy turned away and went back to Sheba, who had remained lying on her blanket gazing at the new female. Tony then went into the enclosure, sat down and started talking gently to Baby, calling her name. He said that he would not, at that stage, go into the sleeping quarters and thus 'force' himself on her but would wait for Baby to come to him. He thought that she might relax better with just one human, a male, as she had always been used to male zoo keepers. About half an hour later, I walked down to the ocelot's enclosure to find that Baby had come out of her sleeping box and was beside Tony. She was still spitting, but it was becoming half-hearted. I had brought with me a bowl of milk, diluted with water as she was not used to all milk, and I gave it to Tony to give to her. Tony placed the bowl beside Baby, who sniffed it and then began to drink noisily.

I asked Tony whether she was responding to his calling her but he said that it was too early to expect her to recognise her name when a strange voice called her. I thought that at nine years she was a bit too old for the name 'Baby', and suggested we changed it while she was with us. Tony agreed and after some thought suggested that as we already had one female ocelot with an Egyptian name, we could call the new cat Cleopatra, and shorten it to Cleo.

As Cleo seemed to be settling down, not pacing up and down unhappily, we decided to see how Snoopy would react to her. We shut Cleo in her half of the sleeping section while we put a collar and lead on Snoopy, shooing Sheba back inside so that she would not distract Snoopy from Cleo and also in case there was a fight between the females. Tony opened Cleo's door and called her. Snoopy, curious as usual, started walking towards the open door, then stopped when he saw Cleo, who walked towards him gingerly. Snoopy remained motionless, Cleo leant forward and hesitantly sniffed the top of his back. Snoopy turned his head and looked at her and then slowly backed away. We felt that as Snoopy was aloof, it was better to put him back with Sheba and Tony spent as much of the rest of the day as he could with Cleo and by early evening, she was sitting on the ground by him, with her two front paws on his lap. Tony told me to try to rub her under the chin as she liked that. I hesitated, wondering if I was going to be bitten, but Tony assured me that she would not bite. I sat on the ground and began to talk gently to Cleo, who ignored me. I slowly put my hand towards her face, she looked down and sniffed if for a few moments and then looked away again. I reached forward and gently touched her under the chin with the tips of my fingers and as she did not snap at me, I began to stroke her fur, which felt very soft. Cleo stretched her neck forward and I rubbed my nails along it and down to her chest. I did this again and then Cleo started to make a low, rumbling sound in her throat and as we did not know her and therefore were not sure whether this meant pleasure or otherwise, we thought it best for me not to touch her again for some time.

After Tony had left the enclosure and had gone into the house, I again walked to the enclosure to see how Cleo was settling down and found that she was lying on the one piece of bare wooden board which was not covered by the blankets. Then I realised that she had never lain on soft bedding before and did not know what the blankets were for – obviously it would be impossible for a zoo to provide blankets for their animals. I enticed her out of the sleeping box with a saucer of milk and water and while she was drinking it, I pulled the blankets over the bare boards. When she had finished drinking, she went back into the sleeping box and this time lay on the blankets, which she has continued to do ever since.

During the next few days, we spent as much time as we could with Cleo and gradually her whiskers stopped moving forward to the 'alert' position whenever we went near her. Tony put Snoopy with her again, shutting Sheba away, but he ignored her as he was still far too interested in Sheba, who was in season. Cleo continually went up to Snoopy, rubbing herself against him, but he moved away every time. She then tried rolling on her back at Snoopy's feet, but he gazed into the distance ignoring her.

About a week later, Cleo went into season, so we again put Snoopy with her. Sheba had by this time come out of season, her back and neck badly mauled from the mating and was chasing Snoopy away, snapping at him if he came too near. At last Snoopy began to nuzzle Cleo and shortly after they mated. They were so engrossed in each other that Tony and I were able to watch and film their mating on our Akai portable video tape recorder. That evening, Tony gave a lecture on our animals to a local Ladies' Guild and illustrated it by showing the video tape recordings, on a television set, which included that day's filming. Wickedly, Tony had not erased the scenes showing the ocelots' mating and every detail was evident. I felt embarrassed and looked round to see now the audience was reacting. I saw that some of the more severe looking elderly ladies were sitting with their eyes tightly shut, their lips pursed, a shocked expression on their faces at the 'sexual exhibition'.

When Cleo came out of season all was quiet and as Sheba is normally non-aggressive, Tony decided to see how the two females would react to each other. He shut Snoopy away and let Sheba out into the enclosure, then Cleo. The two females sniffed each other and then settled down in the sun together, snoozing. Snoopy started to yowl, so Tony let him out as well; Sheba and Cleo awoke, lifted their heads and glanced at Snoopy once, then went back to sleep, ignoring him. The only trouble occurred at feeding times. Snoopy always took Sheba's food if he could, but when he tried to take Cleo's, she stood her ground and raised a paw to strike him, claws unsheathed. Snoopy backed and made no attempt to snatch her food. Soon, whenever Cleo saw Tony approaching carrying food, she chased the other two ocelots away so that she could be first by the enclosure's entrance. In fact Cleo became the 'boss-cat' of the colony, keeping Snoopy in his place and not allowing him to take liberties with her. Sadly, after sixty-five days, Cleo aborted which we attributed to her advanced age.

One day, about four months after Cleo's arrival, I went into the ocelot's enclosure to find that she was crawling along the ground, dragging her back legs, her head twisted to one side. She was sharing sleeping quarters with Sheba as Tony felt that the two females needed a rest from Snoopy. I called Tony and together we managed to carry her into the house. Tony telephoned the vet. who, after examining her, diagnosed brain damage. He thought that her eye-sight had been affected too as one pupil was at a different angle to the other and she was continually sniffing her way around, which she had not done before. We made Cleo as comfortable as we could, placing her box by a radiator and, as the vet. suggested, kept the electric light from shining directly in her face. Tony began to massage her neck and over the following months managed to 'untwist' it until it was almost back to normal.

With rest and quiet Cleo gradually improved until she was able to dig her front claws into the window ledge and pull herself up and on to my typewriter table underneath the window. As she is an old cat we decided to keep her indoors for the winter and during this time, she became extremely tame. She sometimes used a toilet tray and like the other ocelots, wiped and dried her bottom by scooting along the floor afterwards on her haunches. She also sprayed urine round the room, like a male, which Sheba had never done, but this may have been because Sheba had been domesticated, unlike Cleo who was a zoo animal.

Like the other female cats, Cleo formed an attachment to Tony and to show this, she would spray urine on his clothes, never on mine, at least not at first. If Tony left his coat on a chair, Cleo would pull it on to the floor, and I would sometimes find it in her sleeping box, together with his socks. Cleo was still cautious of me, but gradually I began to win her confidence, as with our other females, by giving her food. The only exception is Poppet Leopard who will take a tasty titbit from my hand, eat it and then immediately snarl at me. Whenever I make myself a cup of coffee or snack to eat and drink in front of her, I always, without fail, give Cleo milk or a titbit at the same time. Gradually she began to rub herself against my legs as well and when she began to spray urine on me, I knew that we were friends!

Tony and I do, of course, keep old clothes to wear when we are with the animals but even so, I did not like being sprayed. I soon learnt to recognise the signs indicating that Cleo was about to spray me. She would back up to me, her bottom would rise in the air and her tail would become erect and curved at the end like a shepherd's crook. The noise of her spray sounds like a scent spray being pumped. When I saw these signs, I gently, but firmly, pushed her bottom down until now I am no longer sprayed and she winds herself round my feet instead. Like the other ocelots Cleo rubs her back feet along the ground, in a 'marking time' movement, when she is pleased. Still she did not respond when we, especially Tony, spoke to her. Then one day, I accidentally made a loud noise. I looked at Cleo to reassure her that all was well as I knew that our other animals would have heard the noise and looked round to see what had happened, but she had not heard and was still snoozing. A little later, I stood on a chair to adjust a picture on the wall and as I stepped down on to the carpet noiselessly, Cleo looked round at me, startled. She must have felt the vibration of my foot landing on the floor. I wondered then if she was deaf, but to verify this, I tapped a cup loudly with a spoon behind her; she did not hear. I then realised that she had the same sad and anxious look in her eyes, sometimes defensive, which I have seen in the eyes of some deaf humans. Now Tony and I are always careful to ensure that she sees our hands first before we stroke her because we know that she will receive a shock if an unseen hand suddenly descends on her without first a warning.

Like other ocelots, Cleo is a fairly good 'safe cracker' though because of her illness and age, is nowhere near as expert as young and healthy Brutus. The non-lockable desk does not have to be turned round facing the wall for her as it did with Brutus, though we do take the precaution of fixing a rubber band round the knobs of the cupboard's twin doors. She can pull open the bottom drawer of the filing cabinet however, sniffing loudly at its contents before dragging out on to the carpet things like a pot of glue to take into her sleeping box.

One day, I had been in the kitchen preparing a slimming meal for greedy Willy, who has a weight problem, and after sweeping up Handsome Parrot's seed which Baby Fox had scattered over the kitchen floor after puncturing the new box with his sharp teeth, I made myself a cup of coffee to relax with for a few minutes. As usual, I took some milk for Cleo as I was going to drink my cup of coffee in front of her, but when I went into 'her' room, I could not find her. Then I saw the bottom drawer of the filing cabinet was tightly shut and shaking violently. I opened it to find that Cleo had climbed inside and had somehow managed to pull the drawer closed on herself. She scrambled out and hurried, still a little lopsided from brain damage, to the safety of her box.

Some weeks later, I was rushing to keep an appointment and stupidly left on the table by my typewriter, a bag containing handkerchiefs, gloves and also a mink collar which a boyfriend had given me long ago before I was married. I never wore it being conservation conscious, but at the same time, because of its romantic associations, I had not thrown it away. I returned hours later to find that Cleo had climbed on to the table, rooted around in my bag, rejected the gloves, handkerchiefs and lavender sachet, found the mink collar and had taken it into her sleeping box where she had ripped it to pieces. I found that some of the now tiny scraps of mink were wet with saliva where she must have licked them.

Once, I had a parcel to wrap in brown paper, in which Cleo was mildly interested but not sufficiently to stir from her comfortable position in front of the heater. However, when I began to tie the parcel with string, Cleo became alert and padded over, still walking with a 'list to port', to investigate. Before I could stop her, she had snatched the ball of string in her teeth, turned tail, tripped over the loose end and taken it into her box where she kneaded and licked it. I let her keep the ball of string, together with the other objects which she finds, like a pack of playing cards. For some reason, string seems to fascinate her and she is always eager to have any other balls that I have.

Though Cleo has many soft blankets of her own, especially

since her illness, she prefers cushions, pulling them down from chairs to sleep on near the heater. On cold evenings, after a hard day's work, I liked to sit on another cushion with my back against the radiator. Now I put my cushion alongside Cleo's and we share the warmth. Cleo makes herself comfortable against me, burying her head in my side or resting her chin on my leg. Strangely enough, she will try to push Tony off if he sits there, by thrusting her head between him and the radiator, nudging him away.

When she is relaxed, Cleo sometimes likes to roll on her back, take Tony's hand between her paws, pull it into her and suck his finger like a dummy. She also likes having her tummy rubbed and will roll around on her back on her cushion until one of us tickles her. Tony and I are pleased with the way in which Cleo has become tame after nine years as a zoo animal, where it would be impossible for the animals to have individual attention.

Baby Fox had long ago ceased trying to play with his red and white ball, possibly because he had difficulty in seeing it and was, therefore, unable to co-ordinate his movements to play. One evening, Cleo seemed in a skittish mood; her coat gleamed and, through Tony's massage, her neck had straightened considerably. Tony found the red and white ball and gently rolled it along the ground towards Cleo's paws. It was the first time she had seen a ball, she looked down at it and then tapped it uncertainly. It rolled away, I picked it up and rolled it towards her and this time she came out of her box to meet and push it away with her head and then chased it for a few paces. She then held the ball between her front paws, rolled onto her back and while clutching it fiercely to her with her front feet, 'paddled' it with her back paws. The ball shot away propelled by the force of her back legs and I rescued it and dropped it gently on to her stomach and the game began again. Tony and I now spend many hours playing ball with Cleo. When she wants to play, she pushes the ball towards us and her obvious enjoyment of the game is very rewarding.

Cleo is curious about Baby Fox. She can see him through the glass door running backwards and forwards in the adjacent room. Once, when Cleo had nearly recovered from her illness, Baby Fox pushed the door open and came bounding in, his eyes glittering with mischief, his squint eye only a little askew. He stopped in the middle of the room and did not see Cleo at first sitting in her usual place against the radiator. Cleo's whiskers were back in the relaxed unworried position and then she suddenly jumped forward, like a frog, towards Baby Fox, who turned brush and ran. Nowadays, Baby Fox will sometimes push open the door of Cleo's room, hover in the entrance squinting at her for a few seconds before dashing away. As this particular door has a weak catch, Tony and I always lock it when we go out, even during the day when Baby Fox is normally deeply asleep. Some days, when Baby Fox is safely asleep, Tony allows Cleo to roam around the house when we are there, but she never stays for long in other rooms preferring to slope back to her own den after a few minutes.

Cleo and Willy have met once and tentatively sniffed the air at each other, but I quickly gathered Willy up in my arms because we really do not know if Cleo would attack a smaller animal. My hands have experienced that Cleo's teeth are blunt, but her claws are still sharp and it is pointless taking a chance.

Since Cleo's almost complete recovery, she walks with only a slight roll to the left and she regularly each day pulls herself up on to the window ledge and then on to my typing table, sniffing around for a few seconds at my typewriter, filing basket and me if I am sitting there, before carefully easing herself down on to my lap and then on to the floor. When the weather becomes warmer, and providing she has completely recovered, Tony will put Cleo in the garden enclosure to try to mate her once again with Snoopy.

Shortly after Cleo's illness, Tony parked his car on the mainland and had begun to walk towards our island home when he felt something round his feet. He looked down and there was a small, ferret-like animal. He stopped, the tiny creature continued to run round his feet, so he picked it up, but by its tail not knowing whether it could give him a nasty bite. A neighbour in the car park happened to have a bag, so Tony dropped the animal into that and brought it home. When he examined the creature, he found that it had some shotgun pellets in its back, which he removed.

The little animal was so tame, climbing up our clothes and following us, that Tony wondered if it had been someone's pet and telephoned the police to report finding it, but the police had no record of it being listed as missing. I consulted an animal book and found that it was, in fact, a polecat. I measured it to find that it was over twelve inches long. Its fur was soft with a dark brown mask over its eyes and nose, the rest of its face being much paler with cream-coloured cheeks and fine dark brown whiskers. Its eyes were black and beady, its nose and chin pointed; over the centre of its back and extending down the sides was cream-coloured fur tipped with dark brown; its tail and feet were dark brown and on its stomach the fur was a cream colour with a russet brown 'seam' down the middle. Unfortunately it smelt, discharging a thick, pale yellow liquid, the odour of which reminded me of a farmyard.

The polecat was so friendly, running up to every human it saw, that Tony and I were reluctant to release it to the wild in case it ran up to a human who would kill it. It was no trouble to feed as it ate dead turkey or chicken poults, the same as the owls, together with milk. We decided to keep it until we were able to move house to an isolated part of the country where we would try to obtain a mate for it and release the pair in the garden.

As the months passed and we were unable to find a suitable house, we gave the polecat to an animal nurse, called Pam, working with our local Ministry of Agriculture. Tony and I had met Pam when she accompanied her boss on his inspection of our premises in response to Tony's application for his own quarantine facilities. She was enchanted with the polecat and did not mind the smell. We were so sorry for the tiny creature all alone but felt there was nothing else that we could do for the time being, but when Pam came along, we gave the polecat to her thinking that it would be a pet and have personal attention from her. Pam kept the polecat in her rented flat and made it a tiny harness so that she could take it out into the country for exercise. The polecat, which we called Stinky Mark II, seized a toilet roll from Pam's cupboard, shredded it and took the pieces behind a cupboard where it made a nest for itself. Unfortunately, Pam's landlord, who lived on the premises, did not like the polecat and so a week later, Pam returned it to us. She offered to try to find a home for it and suggested a friend of a friend who kept many ferrets, but Tony and I refused as we felt that we would not want it to be placed in a cage and neglected. At least it was safe with us and several of our visitors were friendly with Stinky Mark II, not minding its, to me, offensive odour. In particular, Julie Browne always asked to see the polecat when she came and spent many hours playing with the tiny creature.

Tony gave it Brutus' blue carrying case, which Brutus had outgrown by that time, and I supplied a blanket. Unfortunately Stinky Mark II had to be kept on concrete because on grass he dug underneath the wire netting guarding him. He is amusing in the way in which he snatches a turkey poult from us, scampers with it into his box, buries it amongst the folds of the blanket and then immediately returns to us to play, running round and round and then climbing up trouser legs until he found that by burrowing underneath the bottoms of trousers he could climb up our bare legs. The first time he did this to me, his razor sharp teeth dug into my flesh, and I shrieked more in surprise than in pain. My cry startled him and he fell down my leg on to my shoe, wriggled out from beneath my trousers, backed away from me for a few paces and then turned and fled into his den to peep out at me a few moments later, with just his beady eyes and quivering nose showing.

Tony and I think we have found an ideal house in the country now, isolated with a walled garden so it should not be too long before the polecat is able to run free, in safety.

Chapter Nine

After much soul searching, we decided to try to obtain a mate for Poppet Leopard, even though Tony knew that in the process he would probably lose part, if not all, of his wonderful relationship with her. We have always disliked seeing solitary animals in zoos and here we were with an animal alone. The danger was that an adult male leopard might reject her because she was not whole, and if there were a fight, Tony would try to break it up and would almost certainly be killed in the process. We thought of artificial insemination and began making enquiries, but discovered that it is only in the experimental stage so far as the cats are concerned, mainly owing to the difficulty of preserving the semen over an extended period coupled with other clinical factors. There is also the possibility that the male might be at risk. Then we heard of a male leopard cub, five months old, at Edinburgh Zoo, which had to be removed from its mother as she rejected him.

The cub had been brought up by the curator's wife for the first few weeks, and then by the girls in the Children's Zoo, where it had moved freely amongst the public. As its eyes had still been closed when it was removed from its mother, and therefore had never seen another leopard, we hoped that it might accept Poppet's three legs as normal. At an early age, the cub had lost its fur. It had never suckled from its mother and was, therefore, given tinned milk, which could have contributed to its baldness. At that time, there was a craze for humans to streak around naked and so a local newspaper reporter christened the tiny, hairless creature Streaker.

Tony travelled to Edinburgh Zoo to look at Streaker and liked him. By that time, the cub's fur had grown and he had a fine, healthy coat. A few days later, Tony received a letter from Roger Wheater, of Edinburgh Zoo, saying, "We do feel it important that this hand-reared animal should go to someone who can take a very real interest in it and because of this we are delighted to let you have him." And so we had a possible mate for Poppet.

After Tony had given Streaker time to recover from the plane journey and to settle down in new surroundings, he attached a lead to the strong dog collar which Streaker wore and led him out into the garden towards Poppet's enclosure. Directly Streaker saw Poppet, he sat down on the grass and gazed at her. Gradually, we coaxed him towards her but when he was a little distance away, he started to spit repeatedly. Poppet flinched and continued flinching and backing away whilst the little cub spat. Tony persevered and although Streaker gradually stopped spitting at her, Poppet always flinched and backed away whenever she saw him. It may be that Streaker's initial spitting reminded Poppet of the leopard which bit her foot, resulting in amputation.

A week after Streaker's arrival, Pam, the Ministry of Agriculture animal nurse, visited us to see the polecat and Tony showed her the leopard cub. Streaker immediately ran to her, Pam knelt on the floor and he nuzzled her for many minutes. As Streaker had been reluctant to meet other people, we think that his immediate acceptance of her may have been because she resembles Ann, one of the girls at Edinburgh Zoo's Children's Section, who had helped to raise him. When Tony collected Streaker from Edinburgh Zoo, Ann, who had become very fond of the little cub during their many months together, was in a flood of tears. She was so upset at losing him that Tony invited her to come and see him, but when she visited us some two months later, Streaker did not recognise her and spat. Fortunately, Tony had taken the precaution of putting him on a lead before Ann went into him and was therefore able to control the spitting and snarling cat.

Despite continued efforts, Poppet still did not want to know Streaker and therefore as it is unfair for him to be a lone animal, we looked for a good home for him with other leopards and in particular with a young female with whom he could grow up. While we were looking for the right home for him, Tony received, as an associate member of The Federation of Zoological Gardens of Great Britain and Ireland, an invitation to visit Marwell Zoological Park, near Winchester. We had heard that Marwell is a splendid zoological park but had never visited it. I thought that it would be the ideal place for Streaker, and Tony agreed and accepted the invitation.

We motored down and as Marwell is not a 'drive through' park where visitors are confined to their cars, we left ours in the spacious woodland car-parking area by the entrance gate. We joined the rest of the Federation party and John Knowles, the Director of Marwell, took us on a tour of the park. He told us that at Marwell, their concept of an animal and bird collection is entirely different in design and purpose to those animal collections to which their visitors may be accustomed. Marwell is not a conventional zoo where animals are seen in small pens and often in a solitary state. Here, both visitors and animals can enjoy relative, but separate, freedom within the park and this may call for new attitudes to animal viewing. Many enclosures require careful study to see and identify every species contained therein.

We walked up to the leopards' enclosure, but I could not

see any leopards. There were none on the ground, then Tony told me to look up in the trees and there high up amongst the foliage, straddling the branches as they would in their natural environment in the jungle, were several splendid leopards, looking aloof and ignoring the humans on the ground. We thought that this would be a marvellous home for Streaker, and decided that when we move, we would build Poppet a similar place among the trees, but not as high, otherwise she would have difficulty in climbing down with only three legs.

We hurried to catch up with the rest of the party who by then had gone ahead to look at some beautiful nyala with slender legs like Baby Fox. The nyala come from South East Africa and their habitat is in low country, dense bush and savanna veldt, never far from water. Being forest antelopes, dependent on cover for safety, they are very quiet and gentle in captivity and accordingly much easier to manage than the nervous antelope such as the impala of the open plains. The nyala at Marwell are the only group in the United Kingdom and are probably the most beautiful and delicate of the medium-sized antelope. John Knowles told us that the nyalas' handsome coats made them increasingly desirable to hunters and this has contributed to their decline. I asked which were the males and was told that their coats are dark grey whilst the females and young are bright brown.

As we were walking towards the paddock containing the only wild horse left in the world – Przewalski's horse – John Knowles said that he believed that in modern society, an animal collection should serve many functions. Firstly comes actual conservation of species and in many cases the breeding of a species in captivity is the only hope of saving it from extinction. With other species, captive breeding is a necessary insurance scheme, in case the dedicated field workers should fail. Education in the *need* for conservation is another vital function, and it was John Knowles' hope that by showing visitors the park's groups of rare animals, many of which were already breeding, it would help them to appreciate the necessity of conservation.

We reached the paddock and saw several stockily built horses with thick necks and heavy heads, their manes erect like stiff brushes, and with well defined stripes along their backbones, and below the knees of their front legs. The Przewalski's summer coat is short and yellow-brown, which becomes longer and darker in the winter. We were told that in the early 1900s, some Przewalski's horses were captured and transported to several zoos throughout the world and that successful breeding has ensured the survival of the species, for the present at least. However, unless zoos begin to co-operate in breeding programmes on a world-side scale to prevent in-breeding, this species may be doomed to extinction. Today, if the animal survives at all in the wild, it exists only in the Tahkin Shar-Naru mountains of Mongolia on the Chinese frontier. We watched some of these fine horses cantering, their coats gleaming in the sunlight and hoped that these superb animals would not become extinct.

We turned round to find the rest of the party were walking over to the tigers, of which Marwell has two species – the Sumatran and the Siberian. The rest of the Zoo Federation party are all experts in their own field, and as I did not wish to show my ignorance too much in front of the others, I quietly asked Tony as we were walking across the grass what the difference was between the two species of tigers in the park, and he told me that the Sumatran is smaller and darker than the Siberian. By then, we had reached the enclosure which is divided into sections for the individual species and I saw that the Sumatran tigers' coats were bright russet and the stripes were closer together and more pronounced than the Siberians'.

I learnt that in the evolution of the tiger races, the more southerly the habitat of each race became, the smaller the animal became and the more dark the background orange colour and the more pronounced and closer together the stripes. The Sumatran tiger is the smallest but one of the tiger races, the smallest being the now almost certainly extinct Javanese tiger. The Siberian is the largest, with many males thought to be as large as the now long extinct sabre-tooth tiger. The other races of tigers come somewhere between these, both in size and coloration.

We were taken behind the public screen into the passageway in front of the sleeping quarters, which seemed to be full of Siberian cubs, and were told that there were two families there – two mothers, the one father and two cubs from one female and three cubs from the other, born about a month apart that spring. All the cubs came to the wire mesh, competing for our attention, then the mothers and finally the huge father, which rubbed himself against the wire by John Knowles. I remarked that they were very friendly and John said he was convinced that the Siberians are so different that they have an affinity with man. Tigers generally have, in the past, had a poor and totally wrong image. They are not savage killers, but noble predators which deserve better of mankind than they have received to date. In John's experience, tigers, like humans, unless they had had personal experience to make them feel differently, rather enjoy human company and will take pleasure in a conversation with people they know, more than most of the cat family. This is by no means confined to those that have been hand reared and is particularly true of Siberians.

Some years ago, in East Germany, John had met a male Siberian tiger which had been caught in the wild as a youngster and was just as friendly as any others he had known. He felt that the reason for this may be the fact that until recent times, from an evolutionary time perspective, the Siberian had little contact with man compared to his more southerly cousins which inhabited densely human populated areas like the Indian sub-continent. One has only to think of the remarkable lack of fear of man that Darwin found amongst other populations which have been isolated from man for various reasons. In other words, only contact with man produces evolved fear, suspicion and dislike; in fact it makes one feel rather ashamed.

Silently, we watched the tiger cubs playing for a few moments, and then the male tiger came up again to John Knowles making a sound which is best translated into English as fuff fuff, to which John responded with the same sounds and told us that this was the most frequent and friendly conversational noises made by tigers to friends, both human and animal. This noise is generally thought to be made by the emission of air from the nose and mouth, though John had never quite satisfied himself about this. However he did assure us that it is a standard greeting which indicates friendship and good intentions between both parties and he uses it not only with the park's own tigers, but with tigers that he has never met before, and has seldom been rebuffed. I asked if the sound ever varied and I was told that the sound was used very expressively and tone is clearly important. For instance, loud and prolonged fuffs will indicate great warmth, as, for example, when friends have not seen each other for a long time, or a sporadic fuff can be delivered in a rather absent-minded way so as to indicate "I am glad to see you, but right now I am preoccupied by wanting to doze or bathe, or watch for the meat truck".

The most intimate sound is a deep 'aaar' which comes from the throat and is accompanied by either rubbing against one's person, or rubbing, as a domestic cat does, as close to the friend as the enclosure barrier will permit. This is an almost sensual form of conversation and only occurs where there is real intimacy. It is important to remember that tigers do not communicate only by sound. Their faces are wonderfully expressive and they are just as capable as any human of indicating mood or intent by expression and these expressions combine use of eye, nose, mouth and most of all ears. Interest, pleasure, displeasure, absent-mindedness, suspicion, defensiveness, all are written on a tiger's face and consequently a conversation between human and tiger must take these subtleties into account. John said that his side of a conversation with a tiger is partly a response to their own sound, they are very tolerant of poor imitators, and general use of human language, from which they understand more than one might at first suppose. I asked if they recognised their own names and was told that the use of names is important and, as with us humans, they enjoy the sound of their own names, but they also know the names of other tigers and some humans.

The most particular favourite at Marwell Park is a male Siberian that John and his wife reared from birth. They and his other human friends have always called him Tiggy or Tig and these are the names to which he responds, but he has an official name which is Miko which is on the front of his pen. So inevitably many would-be friends, who are among the visitors, call out to him "Miko, Miko!" Tig knows perfectly well who they mean, but he usually ignores them, though occasionally he has been seen to throw a withering look as though to say, "Don't try to get on first name terms with me for the price of one admission ticket". Conversations are often quite lengthy with tigers, but depend on the mood of both parties. Tigers are not fooled by duty visits, and indeed do not always themselves want to abandon their current pre-occupation for a chat.

I was reminded of some of the stories, told in his autobiography by Carl Hagenbeck, the director of Stellingen Zoo in Hamburg when it opened in 1907. He had a friendly relationship with his animals, especially with his favourites, the big cats, even when they had been long separated. One tiger which, as the result of a bad cold, developed an eye condition that made him nearly blind, was daily nursed by the zoo director and completely recovered. He and his mate were sold to the Berlin Zoo, but to the end of the tiger's life he recognised Hagenbeck whenever he visited there. "He would always fall into the most violent excitement on hearing my voice in the distance; and when I came up he would purr like a cat, and was never satisfied till I had gone into the cage and spent some little time with him." On a visit which Hagenbeck made to the Zoological Gardens in the Bronx, New York, two lions and a tiger who had spent some time in his care long before, became attentive as soon as he approached their den. They stared "at me like a human being who saw a familiar face but could not put a name to it. But the moment I called out the names by which I used to address them in Hamburg, they sprang up and ran to the bars, purring loudly when I stroked and caressed them." One old lion which Hagenbeck had had for eighteen years so trusted him that, although in pain, calmly lay down as he was ordered and allowed two pairs of claws, which had grown too long and entered the flesh on his hind feet, to be cut and extracted.

Next, we were taken to the American Zone and as we were walking there, John Knowles explained that behavioural and other scientific studies were another need that he hoped the park could serve, particularly as most of their animals were living in as natural an environment and grouping as possible.

The American Zone houses, amongst others, the llama. This animal, together with the South American alpaca and the rare vicuna, are all members of the camel family from Asia and Africa, being descended from the prehistoric camels which crossed the former land bridge into North

America. They are no longer found in North America, but in South America llamas were domesticated by the Incas as beasts of burden and also as a supply of meat and wool. We also saw the guanaco – a wild animal which, even more than the camel, has the unpleasant habit of spitting when annoyed by people or by other animals. I hastily backed away out of range, but the guanaco looked peaceful enough that afternoon.

We went on to the enclosures containing the jaguar which, like the ocelot and other spotted and striped cats, is hunted for its valuable coat. The jaguar is distinguished by the rosette markings on its coat and although it is now an officially protected animal, poaching in the wild still accounts for a continuing decline in numbers. I looked at Marwell's young jaguar, a splendid animal with a shining coat, and remembered that the ancestors of this animal were the models for carvings found in South America, dating back six thousand years. I remembered reading that the jaguar was part of the Mexican Aztec belief. The Great Calendar Stone, made in the time of Axayacatl in the fifteenth century, weighing over twenty tons, twelve feet in diameter and designed to symbolise the Aztec universe, records that the world passed through Four Ages or Suns. The first era, that of the Four Ocelot, had Tezcatlipoca as the presiding god, who, finally, transformed himself into the sun, while the jaguar ate the men and giants who then populated the earth. John Knowles called the young jaguar, named Phoenix, which immediately ran to him to be petted for a few moments before scampering away to play with the young leopard who was sharing his enclosure.

Tony and I left Marwell Zoological Park after a memorable day of seeing animals living in surroundings as near as possible to their natural habitat, and we think that Marwell is one of the finest zoological parks in Great Britain. Unfortunately John Knowles was unable to take Streaker as there was a surfeit of male leopards at Marwell at that time.

As we drove back home, Tony told me that seeing some small buck at Marwell reminded him of the occasion in Africa when he released a similar animal which had been caught in a trap set by an African farmer. Tony released the buck but incurred the wrath of the trapper. Tony forgot about the incident until a short time later when he developed a spot on the back of his right hand which over the following ten days multiplied until his entire body was covered. The spots then grew into blisters, which burst and then encrusted. The blisters were so close together that there was no clear part of his body on which an African threepenny piece, known as a ticky, could be placed without touching a blister. Tony had to soak his pyjamas off in the bath each morning, shaving was impossible, but fortunately the blisters did not hurt. He saw the doctor who took blood samples and did other tests, but eventually was unable to diagnose the complaint. He then sent Tony to a skin specialist, who tried X-ray treatment, but with no success.

Six weeks later, after continued medical treatment, the blisters were the same and still caused much anguish. Tony was almost despairing by this time; eating was difficult, it was easier to drink tea through a straw than from a cup as he could hardly open his mouth and every morning his pyjamas still had to be soaked off laboriously in the bath, as they had stuck to his body. A chemist friend gave him a solution of silver nitrate to be swabbed on and pills, coloured green and brown, one green pill to be taken in the mornings and one brown pill at night; but the blisters remained still weeping and encrusting. Then a girlfriend told Tony about a lay healer called Daisy Jones, a Canadian lady who had lived for many years amongst the Malays. By this time, Tony was beginning to lose hope of getting rid of the blisters which covered his entire body, and was desperate enough to try almost anything. He went to Daisy Jones's house and knocked on the door. It was opened by a tiny lady, about four feet five inches tall with small, dark and penetrating eyes. She looked at Tony intently for a few moments and then pronounced that he had had a curse put on him. She told him that she was busy with a client at that moment and to come back in half an hour.

When Tony returned, the first question Daisy Jones asked was if he had upset anyone and he remembered the small buck which he had released from the farmer's trap. Daisy Jones then went to a drawer where there was a quantity of dried, dark brown twigs. She broke off three small ones and gave them to Tony, telling him to place them in his mouth to be chewed into small pieces. The twigs tasted bitterly pungent. After a minute, Daisy told Tony to cup his hands, spit saliva into them and then pass his hands over his face three times saying each time, "Bismillah", which is Arabic and means 'In the name of God'.

She then placed a tin under the chair on which Tony was sitting, and put some powder into it, which she lit. Tony was enveloped in smoke, smelling sharply acrid, which he had never experienced before or since. The fire continued burning for several minutes, and when it had died out and the smoke cleared, Daisy told Tony to buy a piece of pork skin from a butcher, place it in his left shoe and keep it there for at least a week. All this seemed ludicrous, but the blisters prevented him from laughing. He asked her how much he owed, but she said that she did not charge a fee. Any donations were used to buy gifts for the old people at the Elizabeth Donkin Hospital in Port Elizabeth, where she went every Saturday. Tony was so sceptical that he only gave her a small donation.

When he saw his doctor and also the skin specialist the next day, Tony casually told them that he had been to see

Daisy Jones. The specialist was highly amused, but the doctor said that he had come across faith healers before and kept an open mind. By then, the specialist had ceased giving Tony treatment as it had been unsuccessful and was continuing with tests. Three days after receiving Daisy Jones's treatment, the blisters began, gradually, to improve and within ten days had disappeared entirely. Thereafter, Daisy Jones and Tony became close friends.

One day Daisy Jones told Tony not to sit with his back to the window as she saw danger there for him. A few weeks later, Tony was working late at night in his basement workshop, the barred windows of which were level with the pavement. Suddenly there was the crash of breaking glass and a bullet whistled past his head, missing him by a few inches, and shattering the blade of the hacksaw which was hanging from the wall. Tony threw himself to the floor as another bullet was fired into the workshop. Then the police arrived and arrested the marksman, who apparently had a grudge against him. To this day Tony will never sit with his back to a window and I am the one who always has to take the window seat if we go out, for instance, to a restaurant.

As we continued driving back home from Marwell and just after we had left the county of Hampshire, Tony suddenly stopped the car and ran back along the road. He returned carrying, very carefully, a blackbird which he had seen lying in the gutter, apparently knocked down by a car. As I took the blackbird from him I could feel its heart beating frantically and I placed it safely between two seats.

On reaching home, I found a cardboard box into which we placed the bird, closed the lid, making sure that there were enough air inlets, and placed the box in a quiet room. We have found that the best treatment for such injured birds is rest and peace. I always keep a packet of wild bird seed in the house and I placed a little of this seed in the box together with water.

The next morning, Tony quietly lifted the lid of the box, the bird looked up at him, its eyes bright, then suddenly flew up and out. Handsome Parrot was in his cage just above and was so startled when the bird flew past him that he fell off his perch. Handsome chattered angrily with shock, while Tony carried the bird outdoors and released it. It was a very rewarding moment to watch that bird fly free and settle in a distant pine tree.

In springtime, we usually find some fledgling on the ground unable to fly, and last year it was a baby thrush, with its mother chattering urgently in a nearby tree. To avoid it hopping underneath a shed or the house, where we could not reach it and where it might be eaten by rats at night, Tony found some chicken wire which he turned up on end to make a cylinder about two feet high and eighteen inches across and we placed the thrush in that in a secluded part of the garden, but which we could watch from the house. When all was quiet, we saw the mother bird fly tentatively around the land just outside the wire cylinder and after a time, she flew inside with a worm in her beak to feed the fledgling. She continued to do this throughout the day and that evening, I was escorted by the mother bird chattering frantically as I took her baby to the safety of the house for the night.

Next morning, at dawn, I awoke and quietly replaced the baby thrush in the wire cylinder and watched from the house. After a few moments, the mother bird appeared to feed her young once again until it was strong enough to fly up and out of the cylinder into the apple tree close by and then to soar away into the sky.

The major disadvantage with keeping privately animals such as ours is that Tony and I can never take a holiday away from it all. There is not anyone nearby with sufficient knowledge and experience whom we can trust to feed and care for them properly in our absence. Ocelots in particular need specialised care as they can appear healthy one day and be dead the next, unless one knows the signs that all is not well. Also, Tony does not like leaving Poppet Leopard for any length of time knowing that she would pine in his absence.

I sometimes find the thought depressing that we will not be able to have a holiday for as long as we have animals. When Tony first decided to breed these rare species privately, we planned that even though we would not be able to spend more than two days away – the cats have one fast day a week – we would have relaxing summer weekends in the garden, watching the boats go by on the Thames a few feet away or take a boat out on the river ourselves, sometimes with friends. Unfortunately, for the past two summers this has been impossible because every weekend when the sun has shone, we have been inundated with people, mostly casual acquaintances, who have come to see the animals and spend a few hours beside the river. A traffic warden whom Tony met and talked to about the animals while they were both drinking morning coffee in a restaurant, suddenly arrived with his wife and wanted to come frequently; a man whom we met casually a few weeks before began to bring his two children to see the animals every Sunday afternoon; neighbours bring their guests and it has happened many Sunday nights that I have had to do essential gardening by torchlight as I was due out at work again the next morning feeling tired and jaded after yet another weekend of providing seemingly endless food, drink and talks on the animals to many people. To try to ensure a little free time, we have erected a tall fence and garden gate, which is kept locked, and plan to move to an isolated place in the country soon.

After much trial and error, the food for our animals now

presents no problem; we bought a large deep freeze. I purchase meat from the abattoir and buy a regular supply of chicken giblets, which Poppet Leopard and Baby Fox especially enjoy. The first time I visited the abattoir, I walked into the working section at the back to see a newly killed beast strung up on meat hooks, split open from head to tail, a large pale grey bag, shaped like a melon, hanging out from it. I hurriedly looked away from it and down only to see at my feet another cow lying dead. I quickly walked into the office and as I could not face returning through the killing section, I asked to be let out the front way.

I buy dead male day-old turkey or chicken poults for the owls and the cats eat them too. It is essential for these exotic cats to eat a certain amount of roughage, including bones. Apparently, the Aztecs of Mexico had a constant supply of food including bones readily available for the jaguars and ocelots which they kept. When the conquering Spaniards entered the great Aztec capital of Tenochtitlan in 1519 they saw, in an adjacent room to the cats, projecting from a basket of raw meat a human arm, showing how the bodies of some of the sacrificial victims were utilised.

From time to time, Tony receives requests for assistance in obtaining exotic cats from people who have no previous knowledge of these animals. He received a letter from a haulage contractor living in a busy town, who wanted to buy a cheetah to keep in his back garden. Tony replied refusing to assist and saying that he thought it unfair to such a cat which, as the fastest cat in the world, needs a very large area in which to exercise, far bigger than that which the gentleman told us he had available.

A young married lady called Wendy telephoned to say that she had always wanted a lion as a pet, could Tony help her find one? Wendy said that she and her husband were living in a flat at the moment, where the lion cub would be initially, but hoped to move to the country. She also told

Tony that she had only previously kept ordinary domestic animals and she had never had any experience with any of the big cats. Tony told her that he considered such animals were not for amateurs, but for the professionals who would instinctively watch for the symptoms of illness, often unapparent to the inexperienced, and also for signs of aggression. He went on to remind her that a cuddly cub would rapidly grow into a powerful animal capable of killing a human and that he thought it unfair for such an animal to be kept initially as a pet, probably spoilt, and then rejected when it became too large and the owners were unable to cope with it. Tony continued to try to dissuade her, but she was adamant that she wanted a lion. Eventually, he told Wendy that even with all his experience of exotic pets, he would never keep a lion and said that he would not help her obtain one.

A disadvantage with our animals is that their smell tends to taint our clothes and therefore Tony and I keep old trousers and shirts especially for wearing with them. The cats are very clean, but it is the polecat and fox which are the main culprits. It has happened that I have spent most of the afternoon mucking out the enclosures, disregarding the time, until I suddenly realise that the shops are about to close and I need provisions. I have dashed out, in my old animal clothes, smelling of Eau de Polecat/Fox and after visiting several shops have looked round to see that I am attracting the neighbourhood dogs and leading them as the Pied Piper of Hamlin led the rats!

On one occasion, Tony ran out of cigarettes and went to a local pub to buy some more, still wearing his old trousers round which Sheba and Cleo, both in season, had been rubbing themselves that afternoon. As he stood at the bar, the pub's tom-cat approached and began sniffing his trousers, then rubbed himself continuously against them purring loudly. Tony automatically patted the cat and then went on talking to the barman. Suddenly, the tom-cat hooked his front claws into Tony's leg and began paddling with his back legs at the same time biting hard. Tony had difficulty removing the cat to the sound of laughter from the rest of the bar – unfortunately I was not there! We can ony think that the tom-cat was attracted by the smell of Sheba and Cleo in season and his attack drew more blood and his bites and scratches were far worse than Tony has ever experienced with any of our bigger cats.

Recently I accompanied Tony to see our doctor. We both, of course, changed out of our animal-soiled clothes and were wearing garments which the animals had never seen. Tony went in to see the doctor alone and as he was the last patient I was left by myself in the waiting-room. The receptionist came into the room and remarked on the horrible cat-like smell. She flung open the windows and went into her office. I inwardly groaned because I had been meticulously careful to ensure that the animals had not touched our fresh clothes, then I remembered that the one thing which I had not changed was my handbag. Cleo had sprayed urine on it, in affection, and Tony and I had become used to its smell.

That evening, as I was scrubbing the offending handbag, Baby Fox woke up as usual at about eight o'clock to walk sleepily around looking for a snack before going back to sleep again for a couple more hours. He tottered to the kitchen door, yawning, his squint eye watering, and I said hallo to him. Handsome Parrot heard me and immediately mimicked my 'hallo' like an echo. Baby Fox stopped yawning and looked around puzzled for the other 'human' greeting him.

Many times, when I am gardening, I will look up to see Willy Domestic Cat walking daintily towards me to stalk my moving hands for a few minutes before suddenly pouncing, but only to lick my fingers after which she will sit, like a Buddha, motionless, except for her eyes following my working fingers. She does not venture near Poppet by herself, but occasionally Tony picks her up and sits with her by the leopard's enclosure. In the past both animals have been interested and were just content to look at one another, but on the last occasion, Poppet Leopard licked Willy's face through the wire. The black cat spat and poor Poppet flinched, then turned tail and dejectedly hobbled away on her three legs into her sleeping quarters and would not come out again until after Willy had retired to another part of the garden. The two cats have not met since.

Willy is now fifteen years old and with age, one whisker has grown white and thick, while the other whiskers remain black. Tiny white hairs have appeared on her chest, in the shape of a triangle, her eyesight and hearing are still keen, though she walks slowly and stiffly now; but she can still sometimes be tempted to play with a twig or cotton reel and will move skittishly for a few steps when the wind is wild.

Chapter Ten

Last November, after a particularly wet summer and autumn, many rivers in the South of England overflowed, including the Thames surrounding our island home. We were not worried at first because the river, especially at the back of the island, had often overflowed before to flood the bottom of our garden only, which is on a lower level than the rest. But after a couple of days, we realised that this time it was to be different. The rain was still falling continuously, as it had been doing for many days, and the river at both the front and rear of the island was exceptionally high to within a few inches of the top of its banks. For many hours we watched particularly the river at the back of the island, racing and swirling, almost level now with the gardens. Then suddenly, without warning, an extra volume of water rushed downstream and the backwater broke its banks and came spilling into the neglected orchard outside our garden gate, which looked even more shabby during this harsh month now that most of the leaves had finally fallen. For the rest of that grey, cold day the orchard resembled a miniature lake and we awoke next morning to find that, overnight, it had grown into a vast and menacing expanse of water, hourly increasing its threat to overwhelm us. We felt so helpless before it.

The River Thames at the front of the island raced towards the sea, but was still contained within its banks; a lone duck, which had unwisely ventured into the water, was swept downstream, vainly struggling to reach the bank. The weir, about a hundred yards away downstream, normally quiet, was now a mass of leaping and foaming water; mini waves jostling at its entrance before crashing to the whirlpool below, then to speed, almost as swiftly as the main river, round the back of the next island. At this time, the most dreaded sound was the rain beating like drums constantly on to the roof of the house, yet more water for the already swollen rivers and saturated land.

The water rose rapidly that day. Tony had driven a stake into the back lawn to gauge the water level and every half hour he checked it. By nine o'clock that night, the river was lapping at the entrance to the ocelots' compound. Snoopy and Sheba were in one half of the sleeping quarters, with Brutus alone in the other section. The sleeping hut is raised off the ground a couple of inches, but during the next three hours the river rose so rapidly that the ocelots were paddling in the water. Tony called me to help him evacuate the animals into our house on stilts. The night sky was dark with heavy rainclouds; no moon nor stars were visible; the strong wind blowing off the river was snatching powerfully and persistently at our clothes and the cold rain was still falling. I could feel the chilling water through my thigh boots, which were cumbersome causing me to miss one of the steps down into the lower garden and I slipped. A large honeysuckle bush was near enough to clutch to save myself from falling, head first, into the icy water. I fumbled, found the bush and managed to steady myself, but in doing so the torch, so vital, fell into the water with a sickening splash. I felt afraid. Tony and I were by ourselves, in the black night, wading through river water now rapidly gathering momentum, to rescue frightened animals.

Brutus was pacing up and down frantically yowling all the time, in unison with Snoopy and Sheba. The lights from the house were just sufficient for us to see the cats to safety and Tony and I constantly talked to reassure the ocelots while we lifted into position a small portable wire carrying case to transport first Brutus. I placed a piece of meat on the base boards of the case to entice him. We opened the shed door, held the case up to it above the water and Brutus, who was familiar with this box, rushed inside. We carried him into the house and went back for his parents. Snoopy and Sheba had stopped yowling and were sitting together on top of Sheba's sleeping box, watching the water rising and looking very unhappy. As we knew that the two male ocelots would fight each other, we felt it better not to have Snoopy in the house as well as Brutus if it could be avoided. Tony had recently purchased some large wire panels, the outside frames of which were about two inches thick. We carried seven of these into Brutus' vacated section and piled them on top of one another. Tony then laid some pieces of wood on top, together with a sleeping box, some dry blankets and food and water. He then snipped sufficient of the wire grid in the wooden partition between the two sections of the hut to allow Snoopy to come through. Snoopy, greedy as usual, saw the food, dived for it and while he was eating, Tony started to secure the grid; but before he could renail it completely, Sheba had pushed her way through. Immediately there was a fight over the food and as usual, Snoopy was mean with Sheba, never allowing her any if he could prevent it, even though he was always well fed. Snoopy chased Sheba to the door, she fell out into the flooded compound and began swimming around. As ocelots, like their cousins the tigers, enjoy swimming, we had no fear of her drowning and directly we held open the portable case, above water level, Sheba leaped into it. We carried the dripping and shivering cat into the house, let her out of the case and she allowed us to rub her with towels. Then we coaxed her back into the box filled with dry bedding and turned the fan heater on her, which appeared to mesmerise her. While Sheba was drying, Tony gave her some food and milk, after which she snuggled down and went to sleep.

During all this, Brutus was becoming anxious and after we had dried his wet paws and fed him, we placed him in a large teak box near his mother in the kitchen so that he could see her. When we went to check on the other animals, we found Snoopy stretched out on his dry blankets washing himself and as the platform was about a foot above water level, we left him alone for the night. If the river did rise over twelve inches during the remainder of the night, Snoopy could always jump on top of his two foot high sleeping box and we would check on him again at first light.

Poppet Leopard's enclosure was near the main river, which had not then begun to overflow, but the whining wind, the noise of the heavy rain and the roaring of the nearby weir were upsetting her. Tony went in to her, to reassure and cuddle her for about an hour before she was quiet and went to sleep. The polecat was in a hut near the house, which was also dry, and the owls were on their high perch, out of reach of the flood waters.

Just after dawn, we awoke to look at the water level and found that the river at the front of the island had broken its banks and was flowing into the garden. During the morning, the river moved slowly but steadily towards the house, then underneath it, swirling round the concrete stilts and on to meet its tributary at the back of the island. A minute current appeared in the water drifting along the garden path, together with a tiny waterfall where one of the paving stones had become dislodged and risen a little above the rest. This looked humble enough and yet, at the same time, so full of menace because we knew that the small stream could quickly grow into a huge mass of water capable of engulfing us. There was nothing we could do, we felt so helpless before nature. The nights were to be the worst time, not knowing whether we would wake up to find water in the house. Then that afternoon, the dreaded rain stopped and the sun began to shine, lighting up the last of the summer's roses, the terrifying feeling of menace from the water retreated in the golden light, and the flood waters subsided a little. Sheba and Brutus were content in their boxes with a run around the kitchen and hall for exercise; Snoopy looked smug with all the food to himself in a warm dry hut; the polecat was running around as usual as the water had not reached her and Poppet easily managed, on three legs, to jump over the pools of water in her compound and was fine so long as Tony was near.

Towards evening, the sky again became overcast and then the rain, with all its terrifying consequences for us, began to fall again, heavily and continuously. The noise from the weir grew louder until it was a frightening roar and we could hear the water lapping menacingly against the house's stilts. The police appeared in a boat to take anyone off the island who wanted to go to safety and several families left. Tony and I did not go because of the obvious difficulty of removing frightened animals by boat and because the house is on three feet stilts. During the very bad flooding of East Molesey several years ago, when the Thames had burst its banks as well as the River Mole and we were marooned for two days, the high water had not come into the house but stopped short about six inches from the main floor beams. We did not think that these floods would be as bad as then. Later that evening, the Borough Surveyor and his assistant from Elmbridge Council came to the ait and it was so reassuring that these council officials had come out, at night, to see if the islanders were safe.

That night I woke up several times and listened, despairingly, to the rain still falling hard. Tony went out into the garden during the night to check the water and found Poppet still outside her compound, sitting on some dry concrete slabs. Tony reassured her and told her to go to bed whereupon Poppet turned tail and ran into her sleeping hut, climbed on to the ledge and settled down for the night. Often in the past, Poppet has stayed out in the compound at night, even with snow on the ground, waiting for Tony to go and 'tuck her up'.

The continuous drumming of the rain on the roof and the whine of the wind began to upset the ocelots, causing them to pace up and down. I went into the kitchen to talk quietly and reassuringly to them until Brutus stopped pacing and sat down and purred and Sheba settled down and snoozed. Tony appeared carrying a very wet polecat. She had been trying to scramble on top of her sleeping box, but as this was made of plastic, she had been unable to get a grip and had been slipping off into a couple of inches of water, fairly deep for a polecat. We dried her, found an old cage and placed her in the bathroom. Willy and Baby Fox were sharing a bedroom and eventually fell asleep curled round one another. Cleo stayed in the office and Streaker remained in the lounge.

I arranged for a telephone alarm call for five o'clock the next morning as we were now concerned for Poppet and Snoopy. At five o'clock the telephone operator, who by a coincidence was also an islander, told me that he had been in touch with the police a few minutes before and had been told that the flood warning system was still at amber and was not expected to change to the red danger signal for the time being. Tony waded down the garden and checked Snoopy, who raised his head sleepily, yawned and went back to sleep. The flood waters still had several inches to rise before they touched him.

Poppet, however, was out in her compound and refused to go back into her sleeping hut. Tony went inside and sat on her sleeping ledge, then she came bounding in from the compound, jumped up beside Tony and began flicking the water off her paws, some of which fell on to the thousand-watt infra-red heater high on the wall, making it hiss and splutter. Poppet flinched and backed away, so Tony finished drying her paws with a towel. She then started sucking his shirt and licking his face and after many minutes of this, she lay down, placed her remaining front paw on to Tony's thigh, gave a contented sigh and appeared to go to sleep. When Tony tried to extricate himself quietly and leave, Poppet was instantly awake and began sucking his shirt again. It was about half an hour before she finally went to sleep, underneath the infra-red heater, and Tony was able to leave.

That morning the rain was still falling and our garden was now a lake. The incinerator, in the shape of a standard size dustbin on legs, with a funnel in the lid and sited in the lower garden, had almost disappeared except for a few inches of funnel sticking forlornly out of the water, which had risen six inches up the stilts of the house. With the rise in the water level, our main concern was for Snoopy as his compound was on a lower level to that of Poppet, but we did not have another box in which to keep him in the house, and although Tony could make one, this would be difficult in the flood. We decided to telephone the R.S.P.C.A. to ask if we could borrow a box from them and also to ask for their assistance if Poppet became terrified by the flood. As always the R.S.P.C.A. were very helpful and it was arranged that should Poppet become too frightened, Mr. Miller would come, even at night, with a dart gun to sedate her. We were also told that we could borrow two boxes from the R.S.P.C.A. hostel at London Airport, which is very near us.

As it was essential that Tony should remain at home should the flood waters suddenly rise, it was arranged that I should drive to the R.S.P.C.A. Because the water was now about three feet deep, I wore a pair of thigh boots and, as the current was strong, Tony said he would see me safely to dry land. We set off, easily at first and then the current caught me and I had to hold tightly to a nearby fence and edge my way along that. The water was so deep that I had to walk on tiptoe to prevent it running over the top of my thigh boots. Suddenly my foot went into a pothole, I lurched forward and the river water ran down the inside of the boots to my feet – it was icy.

When I returned with the boxes and also several days' supply of food, Tony told me that we would have to evacuate Snoopy immediately as the water had risen rapidly in my absence. We took the small portable wire carrying box to the compound. Snoopy looked miserable, his paws wet. I wondered if he would refuse to go inside the carrying box as he had not used it before, but directly Tony held the door open, he jumped inside. We carefully carried him out of the compound, but he was so heavy that I had difficulty in keeping my end of the box above the water, which was now almost up to the top of my thighs in the lower garden. Snoopy sat motionless through all this. Once in the house, Tony turned the electric fan heater on to him, but unlike Sheba, Snoopy was frightened of it, so Tony turned it off and dried him with towels.

While we were carrying Snoopy into the house, Poppet had been constantly calling Tony using her 'owl' sound. Tony found her out in the compound sitting on the ledge which he had especially built high so that she would have an uninterrupted view of the river and boats. Poppet jumped down to greet Tony, the water came up to the middle of her legs, she floundered but Tony reassured her and she jumped back to the compound ledge. While she was there, Tony found a long plank and with it made a ramp leading from her sleeping hut to the compound ramp and ledge. When Tony had built Poppet's sleeping hut, he had incorporated a wide step just below her large sleeping ledge, in case she had difficulty in leaping up and down with only three legs. Now, the new ramp ran directly to this step so that Poppet would not have to go into the water, of which she was so nervous. The ramp was supported in the middle by Brutus' blue carrying box and by a small stool at the end. Tony coaxed Poppet down the new ramp, but suddenly she saw the blue carrying box. She froze, staring at it, then spat continuously refusing to move. Tony put his arms around her and gradually inched her over the box, talking quietly to her all the time.

The next time that Tony went to see Poppet, he found that she had safely negotiated the ramp and blue box and was sitting on her compound ledge snarling at the horizontal tree trunk, which is normally her scratching post. We can only think that with just the very top of the moving trunk showing in the rapidly deepening water, she thought it was a crocodile.

During the rest of the evening the rain continued, and not surprisingly the telephone was out of order. The next day, the water round the house deepened and towards mid-morning, our friends Colin and Tisha Browne, together with their daughter Julie, arrived to see if we were safe as they had been unable to reach us on the telephone. They used a punt across the orchard, now a wide lake, through the garden gate and up to our front door, bringing milk and other supplies, and Colin took some photographs of the devastation.

We had stuck a safety pin in the woodwork of the steps up to the house to act as a water level marker and towards evening the water gradually dropped below the pin. Then Sheba broke out of her box. It was made of hardboard and I failed to notice against the dark wood, that she had knocked over her full dish of water several times. The water had soaked through the floor of the box and softened it so that she was able to tear it to pieces. She was intelligent enough to knock the box on to its side and walk out of the gaping hole into the kitchen. I found her amongst the vegetables eating a piece of celery. I quickly took the polecat in its cage from the bathroom, removed all the breakables, before shutting Sheba inside, while Tony replaced the bottom of her box with a stronger piece of wood. As she was very quiet, we left her loose in the bathroom with the door of her box open for her to sleep in.

The next morning, I drew back the kitchen curtains to see, with tremendous relief, the lawn once more, or to be more precise, mud with a few blades of grass sticking through, but the water was still deep enough for thigh boots in the lower garden. The awful and depressing business of clearing and cleaning up would soon begin; scraping mud off valuable pieces of equipment, some of which had taken years to accumulate, to see what could be salvaged and what was now useless; what had been swept away in the strong current; drying out to prevent rust and rot setting in; the garden ruined by its thick blanket of mud. Yet, as I looked, saw here and there, a few plants, some small, which had not been overwhelmed by the devastation and were bravely reaching upwards through the mud.

Chapter Eleven

It was many months before Cleo recovered and as we only have room for two animals in the house at a time, we were unable to follow our normal practice of Snoopy, Sheba and Brutus taking it in turns to live with us for a short while. Streaker was the other animal in the house while we tried to find a good home for him as obviously it would be too traumatic for Poppet to live with another leopard as we had originally hoped. The only disadvantage with Streaker was that he snored loudly and that, together with Poppet's 'in season' noises, which we could hear coming clearly from the garden sounding like someone sawing wood with a blunt and rusty saw, tended to keep us awake at night.

During this time Sheba lost weight because Snoopy ate most of the food, even though we gave them ample quantities for two cats. Normally, we feed Snoopy separately in the enclosure, knowing how mean he is towards Sheba and food, but on many occasions the weather had been too bad for this. So directly Cleo improved and when the weather became warmer, she was put outside in the garden to live with young Brutus. Both Tony and I felt that Snoopy would be too rough for her after her illness, whereas Brutus had inherited much of his mother's gentle nature.

Cleo soon re-established herself as the boss-cat, always being the first to wait by the enclosure gate when Tony fed the cats and chasing Brutus away if he tried to usurp her position. Her coat glistened and her eyes were bright, though she still leant over at a slight angle. The two ocelots settled in well together and at first Cleo followed Brutus around, nudging him with her nose. A couple of days later, Cleo went into season and when we saw that part of her neck bore large scratch marks, we knew that she had mated.

Meanwhile, Sheba was settling into the house, though on the first day she was naturally a little unsure of her surroundings as Tony had placed her in a different room to that which she had been used to previously. As it was a cold evening, I sat on the floor with my back against the hot radiator to watch television and Sheba, after sniffing around the room, came on to my lap and snuggled down.

The telephone is in this room and that night I hid it well, as was customary when Cleo lived in the house because she had liked to rub herself against it. Early the next morning, however, Sheba being much younger, healthier and very active, found the telephone and hooked it out, possibly being fascinated by the ringing noise it made as she did so. I heard the commotion and when I sleepily went to investigate, found that she had bitten off the spiral cord attaching the receiver to the main dialling instrument. But later, when Tony came to try to temporarily mend the telephone while we waited for the engineer, we could not find the spiral cord. We searched thoroughly but it had disappeared and then we wondered if Sheba had eaten it. It was such a long cord that we could not imagine that she had, unless she had managed to get one end in her mouth and then swallowed it like spaghetti. She appeared normal enough and it so happened that our vet. was coming that very morning on his normal routine visit to check the animals.

The vet. examined Sheba and told us to watch for vomiting, when we might have to assist the expulsion of the cord. Tony and I took it in turns to stay with her constantly but after a few days, then weeks, there was no sign of the missing cord. Sheba was very lively, eating and drinking so well that she soon put on weight and was put with Snoopy once again. Eventually the elusive telephone cord did turn up, coil by coil, in the toilet tray and as there was no blood accompanying the coils, Sheba was obviously expelling them without any difficulty.

There is never a wastepaper basket in the cats' room, because apart from it being a splendid ocelot toy, especially when full, to be tipped upside down, kicked around and thrown up in the air, the contents would be fatal if eaten. I read of one ocelot who ate a discarded typewriter ribbon and it was only by a vet., opening up its stomach to remove it, that the cat's life was saved.

Even though we are sure that Sheba had been brought up in a house in the United States and therefore was used to humans, she was not so affectionate as Cleo, who was reared in a zoo and who likes to roll over on her back to have her stomach rubbed. We knew instinctively not to take such liberties with Sheba. Her favourite place was on a high shelf from where she could look out of the window, and she sat regally and motionless for hours gazing into the distance like a spotted and striped sphinx, an inscrutable look in her eyes. Surprisingly she ignored the red and white ball, appearing not to know how to play with it, whereas zoo cat Cleo had immediately begun tapping and nudging it with her nose around the room and would sometimes bring it to us to throw to her.

Like Cleo, Sheba was fascinated by the sight of Baby Fox through the glass door running around, though we kept them apart, as with Cleo, not being sure of her reaction. Once, Sheba did walk into his room, whereupon Baby Fox dashed underneath a sofa to peep out with just his button nose and bright eyes showing, to gaze at the new spotted and striped cat, which made such loud, ferocious sounds.

Sheba is still the noisiest of the cats, as she had been in her quarantine days, far louder than Poppet and Streaker Leopards. One only has to call her name to immediately produce a spine chilling yowl from her, which, in fact, is her way of affectionately answering for when we, and especially Tony, then stroke her, she raises her head to us and shuffles her back legs with pleasure. Tony is her favourite and she will sometimes charge up to him yowling for him to take her head between his hands to rub noses, whereupon she dribbles. I never try to do this as I know that she will not tolerate it from another female. Tony tells me that if I go out of the room while she is in this mood, her attitude changes and she is far more affectionate to him than when I am there.

Of course we have no fear of burglars but our visitors' reactions to Sheba were various. The telephone engineer refused to venture into the room to mend the phone until she had been locked up. Another visitor, a male, stood completely still, like a statue, in the middle of the room whilst Sheba rushed round and round him yowling for him to stroke her. He told me afterwards that he was too terrified to touch her. This particular visitor was unfortunate because just after leaving Sheba's room, doubtless with relief, Baby Fox ran up to him and nipped his ankle in play. He then went into the bathroom and on returning became confused by the various closed doors confronting him. By mistake, he opened the door to Streaker Leopard's room. He did not see the cat at first as it was crouched down behind a box, with just one eye peeping round the corner at him. The man dithered in the doorway for a few seconds trying to get his bearing before it dawned on him that he was in the leopard's room. I called to him to come out quickly, but Streaker, on seeing that a potential plaything was going to escape him, moved quicker. By this time,

Streaker was just over a year old and full of bulging steel-like muscles.

Fortunately, he was at the other side of the room and as he began to race across, his paws thundering on the bare boards, I sprang forward, pulled the man out of the way, slammed the door shut and locked it just as the young leopard skidded to a halt on the other side.

As Streaker had been hand raised from birth and was well disposed towards man, I do not think for one moment that he would have intentionally hurt our friend, but he would have been rough and someone not used to these big cats may have, quite naturally, panicked.

We had tried very hard to find a suitable home for Streaker since his rejection by Poppet, and to assist this, we had decided to offer him on deposit rather than to sell him, but we were still unsuccessful as there was a surplus of male leopards around at that time.

The major disadvantage to us was that he had taken over our lounge and, therefore, our visitors had to be accommodated in the office. One day, Sam, a friend for many years, called to see us. We had not seen him for about two years as he had suffered two major heart attacks and was only just recovering. Sam had always been used to being entertained in the lounge and therefore, he automatically walked towards it. Happily I managed to steer him towards the office in time because I think that the sight of a powerful leopard bounding towards him may well have brought on another heart attack!

The first time I saw Cleo after joining Brutus, she deliberately came up to me and rubbed herself against my leg for a few moments before returning to her comfortable cushion in the sun. We had let her have her own house cushion in the ocelots' quarters because she liked it so much, even though I knew it would be more difficult to wash than blankets. Like his father, Brutus tries to take all the food, so we feed them separately. Due to her age, Cleo's teeth are not very sharp and as she has difficulty in eating large pieces of meat, it is cut up for her into small chunks which we feed her by hand to keep the personal contact. I continue to occasionally give her cream and sardines which she enjoyed so much when she lived in the house. Cleo and I discovered that she relished sardines when one day she climbed, laboriously but determinedly, on to my typing table to inspect my lunch tray, after having quickly eaten the food which I had given her at the same time. She did, however, reject the toast.

Some time ago, Brutus, the young ocelot, was a little listless. The next day, he began to be sick and Tony telephoned our vet. at home because it was Sunday and his surgery was closed. The vet. told Tony to mix Terramycin powder in Brutus' drinking water for the next four days. But when I looked in the animals' medicine cupboard, there was only enough for a few doses. Tony again telephoned the vet. who told us to come over to his home that afternoon to collect some more, which we did and were then invited to the house for a cup of tea.

During general conversation, our vet.'s wife told us that she had been to see some performing dolphins the previous day. On the way out of the dolphinarium after the show, she saw a single dolphin, black in colour and motionless, in a small pool by itself. At home, she mentioned the lone dolphin to her husband who said that it could have been dying and that Dr. John Lilly, the American dolphin expert, has observed that dolphins have been known to commit suicide in captivity.

During the days that followed, I found that I could not erase the thought of the suicidal dolphins from my mind. I would be in a supermarket shopping for food, or washing up, when suddenly I would think how desperately unhappy the dolphins must be in captivity to kill themselves. A while later, we saw Bill Jordan of the R.S.P.C.A. again, on another matter, and I mentioned to him what I had been told regarding the dolphins. Bill said that the R.S.P.C.A. had been concerned for some time and had asked him to investigate. It was not an easy task because those concerned are not very willing to talk, and the dolphins are transported from place to place in the United Kingdom and outside as well. There is a dolphinarium in Holland which is considered to be excellent and where some dolphins are still alive after ten years – the longest living captive dolphins in Europe. There are three separate dolphin pools, the water in which is filtered every hour throughout the day and night. He then showed me the thick file which the Society has on the plight of the dolphins and after reading it, I decided that I would not go to see dolphins perform knowing that man has taken these creatures with a brain as complex as his, from the oceans solely for profit and knowing that some of them will commit suicide to escape from their life 'imprisonment'.

Tony and I are sometimes asked why we trouble about animals. We feel that as animals cannot, of course, speak for themselves to say if they are being cruelly treated or ill, we should concern ourselves with their welfare. Since keeping ocelots and leopards and thus knowing how intelligent and affectionate they are towards humans if treated kindly and well, I am appalled that very many of these animals, and also other species – including reptiles – in the wild, are killed by man not for meat but for the profit from their skins, which are made into rugs or garments, including shoes and handbags to be worn ostentatiously.

I remember watching a film showing seals being clubbed to death, often incompetently, for their fur. At the end of this sequence, there was one film shot, taken on board the boat, of a pile of seals which I presumed were dead. On the top of this pile was one small cub which somehow had managed to survive and was standing, pathetically, on its dead kind. I can only hope that it was killed swiftly, expertly and without pain and terror.

I am told by experts that there are adequate substitutes for the whale, and yet these creatures are still being killed because big business is involved and so much money has been invested in whaling fleets.

Through our unusual animals, Tony and I have met many people who are involved and concerned with animal welfare, one of whom is Bill Jordan, whom I have mentioned previously. One of the aspects of this with which he is concerned is that of experiments on animals. He told me that:

"When scientists don white coats it is as if they enter the priesthood of science where atrocities can be perpetrated in its name and the word 'humane' loses its real meaning.

"Have we the right, moral or logical, to assume that knowledge is good and therefore the ends justify the means? Man's philosophical approach to science is false. For example, if we want to condemn something we call it non-scientific, and to praise it – scientific. Therefore all knowledge which is not scientific is suspect. Thus science is constricted and intuitive knowledge excluded. And in the name of Science, our new religion, man can do to animals what he wishes thereby bringing it into further disrepute."

At the end of January, 1975, the J. Paul Getty Wildlife Conservation Prize was awarded to Felipe Benevides, Peru's leading conservationist and architect of the Pampas Galeras Vicuna Reserve, the Manu National Park and Paracas National Park. Senor Benavides writes, "Between 1971 and 1972, a main U.S.A. furrier sold the skins of 30,068 ocelots, 46,181 margays (very similar to the ocelot), 15,470 otters, 1,939 jaguars and 271 giant otters. New York is not the only destination for this contraband, which travels along an illegal route that starts with unscrupulous hunters of the South American forests. From 1962 to 1969, a total of over 100,000 ocelot skins were exported from Peru, mainly to Hamburg and Frankfurt. The Peruvian hunters received from twenty-five to thirty dollars for each skin, while in Germany the tanned skins brought about ten times that price."

Senor Benavides concludes, "I believe that the ratification of the so-called Washington Convention (on the Trade in Endangered Species) by many countries all over the world is probably the best solution of all, for in the end it requires universal action and determination to end this drain on the world's fauna and flora. Unilateral, or even multilateral, action is not enough so long as there are unscrupulous people willing to buy illegal animal products."

Since the birth of Christ, about two hundred and fifty animal species have died and over seventy of them in this century. Is this century to be known to future generations as the one in which man destroyed so many of the animal species - and also killed so many of his own kind?